THE SUPERTRUCKS OF
SCAMMELL

THE SUPERTRUCKS OF
SCAMMELL

BOB TUCK

THE FITZJAMES PRESS
an imprint of
Motor Racing Publications Ltd
Unit 6, The Pilton Estate, 46 Pitlake,
Croydon CRO 3RY, England

ISBN 0 948358 01 7
First published 1987

Photosetting by Tek-Art Ltd, West Wickham, Kent
Printed in Great Britain by Netherwood, Dalton & Co Ltd,
Bradley Mills, Huddersfield, West Yorkshire

CONTENTS

INTRODUCTION

For over 65 years, the Watford factory of Scammell has been producing commercial vehicles ranging in diversity from that incredible three-wheeled articulated tractor unit to the country's most popular home-produced rigid eight-wheeler. Whether you love them or hate them, the influence exerted by Scammell over the whole haulage scene means that you simply cannot ignore them.

The Supertrucks of Scammell is not a catalogue of their products: it is a tribute to the Company's flagships, the top-of-the-range heavyweights from the first 100-tonner to the S24 and S26. Each is a descendant, yet entirely different in character from its predecessor, and all have taken part in carrying the mantle of British manufacturing prowess to the four quarters of the globe.

The photographs and words which follow recall some of the feats achieved by Scammell in the world of heavy haulage. They can only begin to reflect the skill and dedication of the people at Watford who endow their products with such a stout heart and majestic presence before they emerge through those factory gates.

ACKNOWLEDGEMENTS

This book could not have been produced were it not for the time, effort and assistance afforded to me by a large number of people and organizations. Those specifically I would like to mention are John Banks, George Baker, Michael Bent-Marshall, Frank Bone, Roy Brandley, British Petroleum, British Steel, CEGB, Geoff Clark, *Commercial Motor*, George Dowse, John Fadelle, Lt R.L. Fergurson, Paul Hancox, Dennis Harris, Jack Higgins, Highlands Fabricators, Jack Hill, ICI, Bill Jemison, Tony and Joanne Kimber, Tom Llewellyn, Chris Miller, Judith Morgan, Philip Morris-Jones, NEI Parsons, Howard Nunnick, Arthur Philipson, Alan Simpson, Peter Sunter, Denis Tomlin, Tim Wayne, Maurice Webb and Alan Wheatley, not forgetting my wife Sylvia.

Bob Tuck

It was in 1921 at the Olympia Motor Show in London that G. Scammell & Nephew Ltd first exhibited a truck of their own manufacture. The claim for the new articulated outfits was 7½ tons payload at 3 tons operating costs, and the eager response to this promising proposition resulted in the creation of a new company, Scammell Lorries Ltd. The first cab had a canvas top, an example appearing third in this line; the leading two vehicles have the fixed cab introduced in late 1922. This convoy was photographed on June 11, 1928, leaving BTH at Rugby laden with electrical equipment.

1: PIONEERS AND EXPLORERS

G. Scammell & Nephew Ltd were concerned mainly with servicing Foden and Commer wagons until they exhibited at the 1921 Olympia Motor Show in London, where they offered an articulated six-wheeler offering 7½ tons payload at 3 tons operating cost. The attractive specification prompted orders for 120 vehicles, which meant that suddenly Scammell had outgrown their limited accommodation at Fashion Street, Spitalfields and had added their name to the already lengthy list of British vehicle manufacturers. The following year, Scammell Lorries Ltd set up business in Tolpits Lane, Watford, in premises which they have occupied ever since.

Arriving with the expansion in staff was one O.D. North, a man gifted with ingenuity and foresight and able to produce something different and way ahead of what the others were able to offer. It was North who was credited with devising those first 100-tonners — a concept which was forever to make the name Scammell synonymous with heavy haulage.

Less successful an idea was the Autovan, a small 2-tonner having front-wheel drive coming from a vertically mounted radial engine. The concept may have been ahead of its time, but Oliver North's self belief took a pounding when overheating created distortion and total unreliability. But the vehicle which was to take the Scammell name to the colonies was much simpler and far more successful, with examples still in use 60 years on.

The prototype of the Pioneer appeared in 1927. As its name suggests, it was a trail-blazer, and although it may have been conventional to drive trucks on smooth roadstone or tarmac, the Pioneer was equally at home in dry sand and deep mud, or climbing over boulders, tree stumps and many other obstacles that would deter any sane conventional truck driver. Scammell offered an all-wheel-drive capability with the Pioneers, but in the main they were of 6x4 configuration, either as a platform rigid six-wheeler or as an articulated tractor unit.

The early trials of the Pioneers were awe-inspiring. It was certainly impressive to do a hill start on a 1 in 2 sandy gradient loaded with about 17 tons, but it was the twisting flexibility of the Pioneer that created so much interest. Giant Goodyear pneumatic tyres with 13½ inches section were the source of contact to the road, but the Scammell suspension combined with an innovative transmission was at the heart of how the machine performed.

Even in the early 1930s, Scammell were still offering fitment of their four-cylinder 85bhp petrol engine as an option to the Gardner 6LW, at that time producing 102bhp. The drive went through the normal independently mounted overdrive-top six-speed gearbox to a rear drive, the concept of which was far ahead of anything else devised.

All four rear wheels were driven, but all from one rear differential. This was centrally mounted and powered a pair of conventional half-shafts. These in turn worked through idler wheels to mesh with gear wheels keyed to the four stub-axle shafts. This promoted a positive flow of power to the four driven wheels, but the high movement of their suspension allowed the gear casings to rock on the axle arms, permitting one wheel to be as much as 2 feet above or below its fellow wheel on the same side, yet with both wheels still being driven.

Perhaps just as memorable as the Pioneer's rear bogie was its cooling system. Described as having a special 'still' radiator, it featured a staggered row of wire-wound tubes, providing an enormous cooling surface. Sitting on a shallow top header was a large raised central water pot. This ensured that no matter at what angle the Scammell lay over, the ends of the water tubes were never uncovered. The Pioneers were to operate at altitudes of up to 16,000 feet above sea-level in tropical temperatures, apparently without a single case of boiling having been reported. However, a wisp of steam may well have been a regular sight wafting from that water pot, so it is easy to realize why 'Coffee Pot' was a nickname forever to stay with these early Scammells.

Many of us tend to think of the Pioneer as being intended as a wartime tank transporter, but it was in the Middle East desert where the early models were to prove their worth. At the time, the Iraq pipeline was to be the longest in the world bringing oil to the West. Constructed at a cost of £10 million, the 1,200 miles of pipe ran from Kirkuk in the Mosul oilfield to Haifa on the Mediterranean seaboard. For the transport of this vast quantity of pipeline, special Scammell Pioneers were built for the Iraq Petroleum Company. They were 10-wheeled artics, capable of carrying 10 tons of steel pipes up to 40 feet in length. Carrying a special type of jib crane 24 feet in length, the outfits were capable of self-unloading.

Prior to purchase, Scammell conducted extensive trials for IPC in England over the most testing ground they could find, and so successful was the Pioneer's performance that in total 21 of these pipe carriers were ordered. Lava-strewn Trans Jordanian desert is quite a change from deepest Hertfordshire, but the successful inauguration of the pipeline was a tribute to the design of North and the workmanship of the Watford factory.

Nearer to home, Scammell were trying hard to interest the military in the Pioneer. In 1932 they built MV 5364, which to many was just as famous as 100-tonner *Leaping Lena*, for until hostilities broke out again in 1939, she was the sole purpose-built tank transporter in use by the Royal Army Ordnance Corps, although in fairness, the Royal Army Service Corps had taken delivery of their first articulated low-loaders as early as 1919. These were chain-driven AEC four-wheeled tractors coupled to semi-trailers built by H.C. Bauly, of London, with a potential capacity of 12 tons.

Road vehicles had not featured highly in the logistics of tank movements prior to 1939, the thinking being that they would be moved most of the way by rail and then under their own power as required. However, warfare was soon to illustrate how vulnerable were the fixed tracks of railways, while extensive travel on their own crawlers resulted in quite a high percentage of tanks breaking down even before they had reached the combat zone.

But without the gift of hindsight, the RAOC simply used their lone Pioneer transporter as a training vehicle for Ordnance Mechanical Engineers. Fitted with a power winch, the Scammell showed with ease its ability to unstick battle tanks and self-load them. It was coupling and uncoupling the four-wheeled rear bogie before and after pulling on board which caused most sweat and frustration. The principle of separating the bogie was similar to that used for civilian low-loaders that had knock-out rear axles. However, rather than having separate side jacks to take the weight as the locating pins were removed, the bogie incorporated its own screw jacks, which were moved up and down by sheer brute strength.

Only four of these original-design transporters were built, for it was soon realized that if loading ramps were fitted at the rear and the carrying platform was lifted above the rear bogie, self-loading with these 20 and 30-ton capacity outfits would take only a fraction of the time needed with that well remembered prototype.

In total about 500 articulated Scammell transporters were built throughout the war, although it was the 980 Diamond T ballasted tractor with its six-cylinder Hercules engine which more impressed the Ministry of Supply. With ever changing developments in the size of battle tanks, the capacity and strength of their transporters had to grow as well, so the powerful 185bhp of the American design certainly seemed more fitting for the job.

But tank transporters were not the only Scammell product at that time because about 1,700 Pioneer breakdown tractors were produced, with the British army taking 1,500, the remainder going either to the RAF or for export. Driven via a standard gearbox power take-off, an understandably useful extra to these Scammells was the winch mounted behind the driver's cab. The barrel could take 300 feet of wire rope, which could be used either to extricate the vehicle itself or to pull out other vehicles which had become stuck, although Ray Davison recalled a slightly different use on one occasion.

Ray was stationed with REME at Catterick, Yorkshire, and one night during the winter of 1945 he was called to Allensford, on the A68 road in north-west Durham. An AEC Matador hauling a 25-pounder gun towards Dundee had lost its brakes on the steep descent, eventually coming to a standstill in many pieces at the bottom of the hill. It took Ray and his crew six hours to clear the road and get all the bits of AEC and gun onto the drawbar trailer. Setting out back up the hill for Catterick, the Scammell soon found itself with wheelspin on the incline as a thick covering of frost had dramatically reduced the grip of the fat Goodyear tyres. The hill was only cleared by first chocking the trailer, driving the tractor forward with the winch rope running out, then winching the trailer upwards back to the tractor in true caterpillar fashion.

At the end of the war, the design of the Pioneer was reaching 20 years old. The pressure on Watford had been towards quantity of production rather than development of new flagships, so to meet civilian demand for heavy haulage requirements, the Pioneer had its girth increased and was revamped into the 80-ton tractor. It was now a true ballast body unit as opposed to an artic version favoured for tank transporting, for that sort of heavy loading was far too excessive for the rear axle casings.

These specials and numerous other ex-War Department Pioneers were the main alternative to the Diamond T for heavy haulage work. The Scammells were certainly just as strong and far more flexible in rough terrain, but they were painfully slow. Speed limits in those days were quite restrictive, but being able to do only 15-20mph flat out and empty was rather pedestrian-like progress, although one attribute of the Scammell's specification was certainly effective.

Lennie Sunter and Les Taylor had run into Darlington Forge one day with MUA 461, Sunter Brothers' latest acquisition from Pickfords. Loaded with a heavy steel roll for delivery in South Wales, they were on their way back to Northallerton when they had time to explore the Pickfords modifications in the cab, which included wind-down windows instead of the previous canvas sides. 'What's this', said Len as he pulled a big black knob by the steering wheel. Suddenly there was a loud bang as Len and Les found themselves catapulted into the windscreen; they had just discovered how effective the Scammell hillholder braking device could be. This deadman-type brake was fitted to nearly all the Scammells and was quite a reassurance to many a driver who was asked to grossly overload his vehicle, for its direct action onto the tractor rear axles endeavoured to lock things tight, almost as effectively as the modern day fail-safe spring brake systems.

The next development to the Pioneer virtually doubled its top speed and even enhanced its cross-country performance if that was at all possible. The Explorer was a 6x6 version of the trusted Scammell, but its engine was a Watford-modified Meadows, fuelled by petrol. The change from diesel had been prompted by the military, for historically the army had always used petrol for their vehicles; it was only the navy who had used the heavier diesel oil.

The Explorer was intended primarily as a recovery tractor, and eventually over 1,000 were built during the early 1950s. One of these was tested by Laurence Cotton, of *Commercial Motor*, in June 1952 and he reported that whilst running solo the acceleration of the 15-ton Explorer was exceptionally fast. Even hauling a pole trailer with an all-up weight of 36 tons, 0-30mph was achieved in 101 seconds. Some indication of the spread of performance of the tractor is reflected in that these

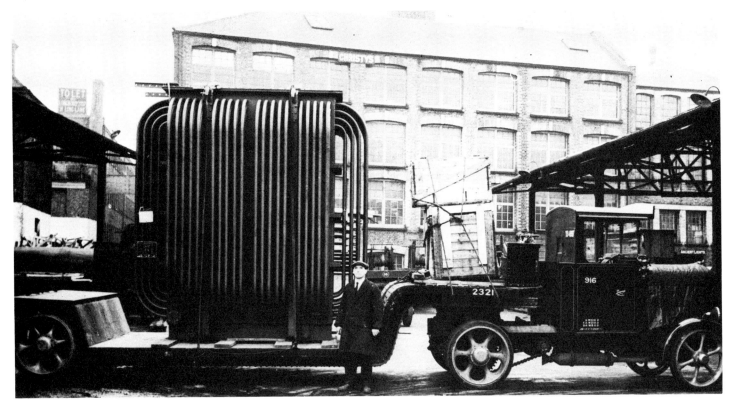

acceleration tests started from stationary with the gearbox in the fourth highest of its six ratios.

Whilst the Explorers were to do their job very well, this was a difficult period economically and Scammell found itself in a weak trading position. They were not to be the only company to be taken over, and at least the absorption into the Leyland empire in 1955 allowed for Scammell's own identity to be retained, whereas Maudslay and others were to totally disappear when taken over by AEC. For Scammell, new backing prompted a new model, one that was to prove bigger, stronger and just as versatile as the Pioneer it was to supersede.

Although Pickfords had made great use of the pack horse, the cart and the barge in earlier days, they very quickly realized the potential of the Scammell low-loader for heavy haulage, an activity from then on always closely associated with the Pickfords name. The quilted bonnet cover on this example suggests the kind of care normally extended to the other type of horse power. The signwriting on the side of number 916 — YU 4997, usually based at Tower Green — indicates an unladen weight for the combination of only 6 tons. This Scammell chassis, number 1129, took to the road on November 17, 1927 and was rated as a 15-tonner. In 1934 it was converted into a 45-tonner by the fitment of pneumatic tyres and a Gardner 6LW diesel engine. Semi-trailer 2321, originally intended as a cable carrier, was used by Pickfords as their transformer float and measured 22ft 6in in the well.

KD 9168, the first 100-tonner, was probably Oliver North's most famous concept, and its arrival in 1929 was to render Scammell synonymous with heavy haulage. Despite its impressive capacity for weight, the Scammell was originally only fitted with a four-cylinder petrol engine developing 86bhp. Three fuel tanks were carried, a small one being located in the dashboard in front of the driver's mate. It will be noted that the semi-trailer hauled on this occasion has only one set of bogie wheels, thus limiting its capacity to about 65 tons. The rear steersman had limited vision round a load such as this locomotive, which was destined for India, but the wooden hut did afford him some protection from the elements.

Double-heading the 100-tonner like this was of questionable value as it probably only raised the top speed of the outfit from 3 to 5mph, still within brisk walking pace for the police escort. The Edward Box vehicles are seen near the entrance to Birkenhead Docks some time around 1947. Box hauled many of these locomotives from Vulcan Foundary, at Newton-le-Willows, and although they weighed anything from 67 to 95 tons, the job was not too testing for the haulage crew: Vulcan crane-loaded them on and, as they were consigned as cargo for the jumbo ships of the Blue Funnel line, their removal was equally straightforward, the ships being equipped with 100-ton derricks.

Pickfords operated the second Scammell 100-tonner, BLH 21, or *Leaping Lena* as she was more affectionately christened due to her lively starting gait when hauling a heavy load. This Vickers photograph clearly illustrates the size and capacity of the machine; even with a 67-ton press on board there is no deflection or bending of the sturdy girder frames. The rear steersman's original wooden hut had disappeared by this time, having proved less durable than the rest of the vehicle, and the Scammell's original petrol engine had been replaced by a Gardner diesel.

The prototype of the Pioneer appeared at Watford in June 1927. This 6x4 configuration, with the front axle undriven, was to be adopted for most of the production versions, but even in 6x6 form the articulation of the suspension across the vehicle was phenomenal. The amount of movement permitted between the rear bogie wheels was also impressive, and was made possible by an entirely new approach to the construction of the vehicle's transmission. One notable change from the prototype made for production Pioneers concerned the design of the radiator, the well-known Scammell 'coffee pot' header tank not having appeared yet at this stage.

It was envisaged that at times the Pioneer would be asked to work in extreme adverse conditions, beyond even its excellent traction ability. Bodywork was therefore built with ample clearance round the driving wheels to allow chains to be fitted, a feature visible in this test shot taken during January 1928. The canvas top looks fairly dated (though nearly 60 years later Leyland were to win acclaim when they fitted something not dissimilar to a very special Roadtrain and called it a cabriolet!) The central location of the narrow cab allowed for lengthy pipes to be carried on each side, effectively stretching the length of the load platform. Even when a fixed cab was fitted, Scammell regularly built in roof hatches as that was sometimes the only way the driver could get in and out.

Above: one of the first large orders for the early Pioneers came from IPC, the Iraq Petroleum Company. They took delivery of 21 of these 10-wheeled articulated outfits which were built to carry 10 tons of steel pipe in lengths of up to 40ft. The pipeline they worked on stretched 1,200 miles from Kirkuk, in the Mosul oilfield, to Haifa, on the eastern Mediterranean coastline. Opposite: Scammell produced their first articulated Pioneer specifically aimed at the tank transporter market in 1932. It had grown in size since the early prototype, the large radiator and larger Goodyear tyres adding to the impression of bulk. Seen here on testing trials, this Pioneer is loaded with a smaller Scammell trailer plus test weights, adding up to 17 tons. A gradient of 1 in 2 on loose gravel provided an ideal photographing spot, but proved of little difficulty to this remarkable machine.

Early Pioneers found themselves utilized for all sorts of tasks, not least as general haulage vehicles. OIA 708 was operated by South African Roadways of Durban and, whilst the cab and bodywork have an obvious locally-built, colonial air about them, there is no mistaking that radiator with its raised water pot.

Orders did not exactly rush in for the Scammell tank transporter. The prototype received the civilian registration number MV 5364 and the War Department number H 22509, and from its construction in 1932 until the outbreak of hostilities in 1939 it was to be the only one of its kind. The outfit was used predominantly for training, and is shown here loaded with a Medium Tank Mk II, more commonly referred to as a Vickers Medium.

1939, however, quickly brought orders for more tank-transporting vehicles. *Snow White* has lost the original stark prototype lines and has a more traditional Pioneer appearance. This semi-trailer followed the original design, but only four of these were built, subsequent versions incorporating ramps over the rear bogie to avoid the time-wasting job of knocking out the back axles for loading and unloading. The Scammell, which formed part of the 1st Armoured Division that went across the Channel in May 1940, is seen in France carrying a Cruiser Mk IV.

21

This REME photograph furnished by Brian Baxter shows the 30-ton capacity Pioneer tank-transporting outfit which formed the main bulk of the Scammells produced for this line of work. It is loaded with an early-model Sherman tank in North Africa around 1942. The exposed driving wheels on the Pioneer meant that, if required, tracks could easily be fitted over the tyres to increase traction in the arduous desert conditions. One obvious drawback to the articulated transporter arose from the fact that rarely did the battle tank become immobilized in a position suitable for recovery. The rival Diamond T ballasted tractor hauling a Rogers drawbar trailer was better suited to this work, for it could simply drop its trailer and use its own winch to drag its intended load to somewhere more suitable for loading.

Back in civvies. After hostilities ceased, thousands of Pioneers were spread throughout the globe. The gun tractors were naturals for heavy haulage work, and it took very little modification for the articulated tank transporters to be adapted as heavy locomotives too. This Pioneer, seen working in New Zealand on August 16, 1948, was run by the Public Works Department of Wellington, and is hauling a BTH synchronous condenser supported on a very modern Dyson frame trailer. The load, which was built in Rugby, eventually reached its destination after a trip down the Otara creek on a raft.

E.W. Rudd was a member of the original board when Scammell Lorries Ltd was floated in 1922, so it was only natural that his haulage company should favour Scammell products. They continued to use steamers for heavy haulage work until the late 1930s, but specially built AJD 140 was a worthy replacement when the coal-burners were phased out. The company was nationalized in 1949 and, although the Rudd name remained for some time, the 6589 designation indicates that the Scammell's use was already being governed by Pickfords, the ninth division of British Road Services, when photographed by J.W. Kitchenham in March 1950 in the Bournemouth area hauling a C.A. Parsons stator on a Rudd-built girder trailer.

Opposite: following a repaint, AJD 140 lost its original owners' identity — the coachline technique adopted by Pickfords, extending even to the ballast box, lends an admirable touch of style. The spacious cab had only two doors, but a driving position close to the centre of the vehicle allowed for the general use of the driver's door even with the outfit in motion. This Scammell was worked by Pickfords until March 1959 and is seen here in Liverpool Docks around 1954, waiting for a Braun column to be unloaded from its Crane solid-tyred bogies. Above: with the early 100-tonners going out to grass in the 1950s, it was the Pioneers that were obliged to take over their work load, even if it meant their multiple use. This resplendent Vulcan Foundry locomotive weighed 99 tons, the fine print on the side identifying it as number 49 in a shipment to Bandar Shahpour for the Indian State Railways. Edward Box was another company to disappear after nationalization in 1950: GKD 56 had chassis number 5751 and was the ex-Edward Box 80-tonner, fleet number 185, at first designated 6262 by Pickfords before being renumbered M350 prior to its disposal in October 1957. Close examination of the trailer reveals that the Crane running gear consists of the bogies out of their well-remembered T3440, nicknamed *The Abortion*, linked to extra long frame girders that Pickfords particularly used for long locomotive carriage. The outfit is pictured *en route* from Newton-le-Willows to Liverpool around 1954.

26

Opposite: this fractionating column, made by G.A. Harvey for American-based oil refinery builders Lummus, was much photographed on its journey across London, but rarely has due credit been given to Edward Box's 80-tonner, HPP 316, which did the haul unaided though the 83ft long load weighed 108 tons, so making a total combination weight close to 150 tons. This Scammell, chassis number 5582, was later to receive the Pickfords fleet number 6263, then M351, eventually being sold in July 1959. Protracted research by George Baker traces its original ownership back to the Forestry Commission. Above: Red House Motor Services can trace their history back to 1911, and although they, too, were nationalized, they set up business again in the early 1950s trading from their current premises in Cromwell Street, Coventry. The company always felt themselves to be at the top of the second division of heavy hauliers when Pickfords and Wynns were dominating the scene. RW 873 was one of the fleet's flagships, usually coupled with a Crane float drawbar trailer, and is seen here during the early 1960s hauling a fabrication built by Davidsons of Belfast.

Above: although currently using Fodens for most of their heavy work, Red House Motor Services have used Scammells extensively throughout their long history. One regularly recurring job has been hauling loads from GEC, formerly BTH, at Rugby. This GEC photograph, dated May 21, 1951, shows the Red House Scammell 50-tonner artic registered YV 3156 (though displaying general trade plates 151 WK at the time of the picture). Fitting pneumatic tyres on the front axle, as well as helping to maintain directional stability, allowed the vehicle's speed limit to be raised from 5 to 8mph. The ungainly extended bonnet suggests that the original four-cylinder petrol engine has been replaced with a longer six-cylinder Gardner during the tractor's lengthy career. Opposite: this Vickers photograph shows Pickfords 7030 and 7032 in Scotswood Road, Newcastle, around 1954. Both tractors were absorbed into the Ninth Division from the fleet of Isaac Barrie. The 80-tonner, DUS 951, chassis number 5753, was to be renumbered M510 and remain with Pickfords until March 1959. It was one of a pair of similar Scammells, the other being DUS 950, chassis number 5752. The Crane solid-tyred bogies complete with table top seen here had a capacity of 200 tons and were to be kept in use by the haulier for another 30 years thanks to their strength and very low running height.

The large financial resources of Pickfords meant that they could often run with the luxury of compatible and identical tractors for push-pull work, the two in this Parsons photograph also having consecutive registration numbers, JXL 219 and JXL 220. They were to be renumbered M168 and M169 in Pickfords fleet list, although their chassis numbers, 6449 and 6630, were not adjacent. The duet are seen taking a C.A. Parsons transformer on a local Tyneside haul to the Stella West Power Station. This Crane trailer, fleet number T5902, had a capacity of 120 tons and the running height of the frame's side girders could be varied to suit the load, this particular transformer having unusually high carrying lugs.

Pickfords also bought ex-War Department vehicles: close scrutiny of the rear part of the cab and the ballast box of the example in this Vickers photograph will reveal detail differences from the factory-built 80-tonners. MLE 539 had the chassis number 5116 and Pickfords fleet numbers 7996 and M593 before being disposed of in July 1958 to make way for the new breed of Junior Constructors then arriving.

In military form, the Pioneer was expected to haul no more than 30 tons payload as an articulated tank transporter. Others were built either as heavy breakdowns, artillery tractors or just general service tractors which could be kitted out with six concrete ballast blocks held in an angle-iron framework. Once bought by the civilian heavy haulier, however, the tractors were expected to move all sorts of astronomical weights. UZ 4716, working in tandem with UZ 4717, is hauling a 115-ton C.A. Parsons stator *en route* to Belfast Municipal Power Station West, the all-up weight being close to 240 tons. The six-axle Crane girder trailer, which was given the Ulster Transport fleet number 4491, is the 200-tonner built for Robert Wynns about 1955, numbered 444 by them, and only superseded when the Dereham manufacturer provided 300-ton trailers for the Welsh operator in 1963.

When originally designed, the Pioneer had been offered to potential purchasers as an optional all-wheel-drive tractor, but it was the 6x4 configuration which proved most popular. The demand for a driven front axle did not arise until after World War 2, when the army asked for even more mobility from a batch of recovery tractors they intended to order. JLR 80 was an experimental tractor built at Watford on a Pioneer 6x4 chassis, with a driven front axle added, and is seen undergoing testing. trials before implementation of the resulting new model.

From the 6x6 experimental Pioneer was developed the Explorer: there was a slight variation in the cab and the height of the ballast body, but it retained the characteristic raised water pot on top of the radiator. To meet the demand for better performance and for compatibility of fuel with other army vehicles, a Meadows 10.35-litre 175 bhp petrol engine was fitted, though this suffered from a fuel consumption which never bettered 2 to 3mpg. Even though cross-country ability was exceptionally good, the winch, which could be operated through the rollers visible close to the front nearside wheel, was a standard part of the specification.

Although many Pioneers were to make the transition from military to civilian use, very few Explorers seemed to go the same way. Two that did were run by Hill of Botley during the 1950s and 1960s, and one of them, TOT 297, is seen in June 1961 outside the Towers Cafe, Basingstoke. The 6x6 Scammell is hauling a 28-ton diving launch from Thornycroft's Woolston yard to London Docks. The trailer is an extensively modified Rogers tank transporter that Hill lengthened and widened specially for this type of load and which was still at work in their hands in 1986.

When not dealing with glamorous heavy-haulage jobs, TOT 297 was expected to earn its keep on more mundane general work. It is seen again in 1961 in the Burt Boltons timber yard at Totton, near Southampton, with telegraph poles hauled from the Crown Land Estate at Windsor. As it was used frequently, Hill re-engined the big Scammell with a Leyland 680 diesel which improved its fuel consumption by nearly 400% compared with the original petrol engine. The steam crane doing the unloading was built by Grafton & Son of Bedford.

Chassis number 3632 was built by Scammell as World War 2 was reaching its peak in 1942. The 6x4 Pioneer was destined to be a gun tractor: very few people would have believed that, 43 years on, the same vehicle would be engaged in house removals. Although many operators were to despair at the leisurely gait of the Pioneer, the slow-speed control was a boon to Watkins, Building Movers, of New Zealand. They are seen here moving a typical desirable residence which, at 40ft wide, was within inches of the limit of what could be hauled without removing any adjacent street furniture. The small signwritten motif on the front bulkhead, *Powered by Gardner*, reflects this operator's high regard for the manufacturer of the 6LW engine.

2: CONSTRUCTORS AT WORK

The Constructor made its appearance in 1952. Although a direct descendant from the Pioneer/Explorer range, in shape, size, capability and potential it was something entirely different, as it needed to be because Scammell had seen their favoured markets slowly slipping away from them. A new product was urgently needed to reverse this situation.

The British army had learnt many lessons during World War 2 about tank movement and they had no intention of being caught out should hostilities arise again. With nothing being constructed by Scammell to replace the Pioneer in the late 1940s, the military had earmarked Thornycroft to replace their varying range of British/American transporters with the Antar. The current vogue was big and powerful, and the first of these vehicles were petrol-powered with the mighty Rover Meteorite engine. Even the Iraq Petroleum Company, who had given Scammell one of their first big orders for the Pioneer, had plumped for the massive Thornycroft, so the men from Watford had to come up with something special.

The focal point of a vehicle for most people is its cab, although there are some who argue that as far as Scammell are concerned the cab is the last thing they think about. The first cab on the Constructor may have tended to prove that point, for in essence the design was very much a hand me down from that used on some lightweight Bedfords that were being phased out of production. In fact the same cab tooling was used in the updated version of the three-wheeled Mechanical Horse when it was rejuvenated into the Scammell Scarab.

Intended for worldwide markets, the Constructor cab had the walls and roof double-skinned and filled with insulation material, and, most characteristic of all, the roof canopy was extended to provide a cheeky little sun visor. Inside the cab, things could be described as either extremely accessible or downright cramped, depending on your point of view, but the cab was so small in relation to the width of the vehicle's chassis that Scammell offered to offset it to the right or left, depending on whether it was a right or left-hand drive vehicle.

The driver sat on a Woodhead Munroe adjustable seat of leather-covered Dunlopillo which, although sounding very grand, prompted a rather erect driving position to peer through the rather small sloping windscreen which, in true colonial fashion, could be opened outwards to allow for better ventilation.

The driver's hand fell naturally onto the gearbox lever implanted through its larger metal gate — a Scammell trademark on all its vehicles at that time and well into the 1960s. This feature indicated very clearly where each gear was located, but it prevented any skip-shifting or jumping through the gears by missing intermediate ratios.

To reproduce a similar 'house-climbing' quality of performance to that which the Pioneer had offered, yet have the capability to propel the vehicle at a reasonable gait when unladen, Scammell incorporated what they called a transposing box onto the back of the standard six-speed gearbox. This comprised an auxiliary two-speed gearbox plus a dog clutch for disengaging the drive to the front axle. In theory, the Constructor had 12 different gear ratios, and although some of the intermediate ones did overlap, it gave the Scammell the ability to move 100 tons of payload up reasonably steep inclines and still reach a respectable 38mph on the flat.

Taking the power to the six wheels, Scammell used their spiral-bevel and epicyclic-type axles coupled to constant-velocity universal joints on the front and separate propeller shafts on the rear, which once again looked nothing like anything else currently in use. The axles were similar in shape to a squat cylinder, but their suspension lived up to the articulation standards set by earlier Scammells and was far stronger than that of the revolutionary Pioneer.

In deciding what to use as a power source for their new Bedford look-alike, Scammell were in a bit of a quandary. They wanted far more power than the 110bhp that was available from the traditional standard Gardner diesel engine, but they did not want to take what they felt would be a backward step and resort to a high-powered petrol engine. Early Constructors were thus fitted with a Meadows engine, although this was soon to be superseded by the offer of the 12.17-litre Rolls-Royce C6NFL diesel, which could produce 185bhp at 2,100rpm and 200bhp at 2,200rpm. It was quite a powerhouse, and it certainly produced a deafening symphony of noise to go along with it.

The new Scammell soon proved to be very popular in all parts of the globe. They were used as tank transporters or recovery vehicles by the military, but probably the hardest work demanded from the Constructor was in the Middle East as an oilfield truck. Used sometimes as an artic, but more often as a long-wheelbase platform six-wheeler, the Scammell regularly had to withstand quite a punishing regime of self-inflicted exercise. Lifting loads of anything up to 30 tons in weight onto the back of a truck when you are in the middle of a desert and any form of mobile cranage is just a pipedream brings about the strangest of solutions. Naturally, the Scammell winch would come to the fore and crude ramping would assist the fight

against gravity, but once the 30-ton mass rested on the extreme rear end of the Constructor's body, the laws of physics and moments meant that the whole front end of the Scammell would lift clear of the ground. True, as the winching continued, the front axle would come crashing back down to where it should be, but punishing tricks like this merely served to underline the high quality of workmanship produced in that distant English factory.

Back at home, the easing of nationalization meant that Pickfords were not alone in showing an interest in the Constructor as a heavy haulage machine. OUR 176 was offered in ballast box form to demonstrate the strength of the new Scammell, but it was soon obvious that the cab was a major drawback. The same type of cab, sometimes without the sun visor, was already in use for the smaller four-wheel-driven Mountaineer, but as these were only intended as 45-ton payload vehicles, their regular crewing of a driver and only one mate meant that the compact cab was more or less acceptable. But with the bigger 100-ton Constructor hauling all sorts of loads requiring more attendants, a type of crew cab was naturally desirable. 1955 saw the roomy coachbuilt product appear, early versions going to Pickfords, who took five of the new 6x6s during the first seven months of the year, having the consecutive chassis numbers 8994 to 8998 and the registration marks PUC 471 to 475. More individual in appearance, and perhaps more memorable, were the two machines that went to the North East at the same time, Siddle Cook's SPT 600 and Sunter's NAJ 920.

A great deal was being asked of the Constructors at this time, for developments, especially in the electrical industry, meant that loads were getting not only larger but, more importantly, far heavier. Massive trailers were being built to carry the cargo and these too were growing in size: the famous Pickfords Crane 200-tonner, TM 413, for example, which was normally based at Birmingham, was believed to tip the scales close to the 80-ton mark unladen. The precise weight was never really established, for its declared licensing unladen weight was always around the 60 tons figure, and there were few weighbridges around at this time which could satisfactorily confirm the facts. Either way, hauling 60 to 80 tons of empty trailer still required a considerable effort from the new Scammell. Put 150 to 200 tons of payload onto the same combination, and it required the classic sight of two, three or even four heaving Constructors working in concert to propel the mass along.

For lighter weights, the power of the Constructor had to be kept in check, as John Robinson, the leading Sunter driver for nearly five decades, recalled. His company was hauling long girders, resting on two independent bogies, through Stockton-on-Tees, and although the town is not high above sea-level, Hartburn Bank meant a very sharp incline on the western outskirts. The natural tendency to put your foot down had to be watched, for one driver who did this with the big Scammell found that so much power was exerted that the hauling tractor pulled the leading bogie forward from under the load, the combination only coming to a grinding halt as the fail-safe umbilical air lines running to the rear bogie were torn in half.

For more delicate operations, a hand throttle was of great value to the Constructor driver, although its use sometimes tended to frighten people who were watching the vehicle's progress. Tees Viaduct, at Middlesbrough, is one crossing where the highway people demand a slow measured pace from heavy loads so that the bridge's foundations are not unduly disturbed. Bill Jemison used to take this opportunity to simply engage the hand throttle, point the Scammell straight, then go to the back of the crew cab and make a fresh brew of tea. After the initial shock, the escorting police motorcyclists became used to seeing a driverless Scammell coming towards them, but they never ventured too close to investigate because it was not unknown for them to be showered with cold tea when Bill threw out the contents preparatory to warming the pot!

Although people like Cooks of Consett and Hills of Botley subsequently used the big 6x6 Constructor in articulated form, in the main its sheer size dictated that it was used for fairly substantial work only. Bridging the gap between a hard-worked Mountaineer and under utilization of the Constructor, Scammell produced the Junior Constructor especially for the middleweight bracket of road-going heavy hauliers.

As the name implies, it was a downrated version of the big Scammell, having an undriven front axle or 6x4 configuration, and a Leyland 680 engine as standard fitment powering through a six-speed gearbox. The leadership of Pickfords in the heavy haulage field at that time is perhaps reflected in the fact that from November 1957 to January 1958 they put 20 Junior Constructors on the road, with 10 more to follow a year later. No-one else could emulate purchasing power of this level, but individual Juniors, with probably the most aesthetically pleasing version of the coachbuilt cab ever built, proved a practical asset to many of the growing band of Pickfords competitors.

Scammell produced these Juniors as required for another 10 years, but a variant of the Constructor that was to stay in production for over 20 years was the Super Constructor. Modestly rated for 180 tons train weight operation, this Scammell's big change beneath the skin was the fitment of the Self Changing Gears RV30 eight-speed gearbox and the removal of the clutch pedal, with a stubby little gear-lever replacing that massive cast-iron gate.

Pickfords put two of their first Supers, WYH 901 and 902, into service in March 1960, these machines having the Leyland/Albion 15.2-litre 900 engine under the bonnet, a power unit which had been adapted from its normal industrial application of powering railcars. As an indication of its power, when Sunters tried the 900 engine as a replacement for the Hercules in their Diamond Ts, it briskly and contemptuously snapped the half-shafts.

The two Super Constructors bought by Sunters had the Rolls-Royce engine, now in supercharged form and producing 250bhp; 447 DPY and KVN 860E worked hard for the Northallerton haulier, but both had the reputation of being engine oil guzzlers. To save time, the drivers had piping running from a 5-gallon drum carried in the ballast box so that at the turn of a tap the sump could be replenished to its operating level.

When it came to Northallerton in January 1963, 447 DPY took over as fleet flagship from the seven-year-old Rotinoff. These two tractors covered all Sunters' big hauls in this period,

The Mountainer was to make its first appearance in 1949. The distinctive front axle, of Scammell design, was also to be seen soon after on the Explorer and on the stronger Constructor range. The model was also the first to make use of the Bedford look-alike cab, and this Scammell, with its clean strong lines, was a natural choice for the lighter range of desert and oilfield work.

the 200-ton ammonia converters taken into ICI at Billingham being particularly memorable. The lack of strong enough cranage anywhere in the vicinity meant that the 60 foot-long West German-built cylinders came back onto dry land 53 miles from their destination at the Walker naval yard of Vickers, on the River Tyne. To surmount the infamous Cut Bank in Newcastle, the two Rolls-Royce-powered tractors were headed up by a Leyland-powered Junior and a Cummins-engined Diamond T; exhilarating stuff, although to drivers like Robinson, Fraser, Corbett and Goulding it was just another working day.

On the national heavy haulage scene, the Super Constructor only had limited popularity when compared to its smaller counterparts. But in more distant climes, the Super took over the Scammell mantle in the oilfields as a recovery/wrecker and a high-mobility articulated tractor unit of massive dimensions; it was as late as April 1981 that the last batch of Super Constructors were made.

But for its last 17 years, the big 6x6 had been forced to share the limelight with another stablemate after an entirely different range had been put into production at Watford which enabled the heavy haulier to move into the super-heavyweight league.

The Mountaineer was also utilized in the United Kingdom, KVN 604 being Sunter Bros' first brand new heavy haulage machine to be bought after the rigours of nationalization were eased in the early 1950s. This British Steel photograph shows driver John Robinson leaving Dorman Long's premises on Teesside on April 5, 1955, with an awkward girder supported on the Crane 60-ton float and destined for Beard Morris, in Glasgow, for machining. The Scammell was fitted with the 130bhp Meadows engine, only a modest output in today's terms, although sometimes Lennie Sunter despairingly wondered why it couldn't haul 80 tons gross up some very steep hills.

The Constructor range was introduced by Scammell in late 1952, and although superficially it could be said to be simply a six-wheeled version of the Mountaineer, under the skin it was a far stronger and more powerful machine. OUR 176 was an early demonstrator put out by the manufacturer, and Pickfords were keen to press it into service rather than use the mature 80-tonners. Seen in South Shields during early 1954, it is hauling the first of three short-circuit testing transformers built by C.A Parsons for Blyth Power Station. With an all-up weight in excess of 200 tons, the new Scammell is being assisted by a pushing Mountaineer, registered NGF 119.

Once a bigger driving cab had been created, Pickfords were soon to bring the new Constructor range into their fleet. Chassis number 8994 was their first 6x6 purchase and was registered PUC 471 when put to work in February 1955. It was given the fleet number 8931 at the outset, but following a vogue of renumbering, its new designation was M1007. The vehicle is seen around March 1964 coupled to the Crane 200-tonner, and is about to lose its load on Newcastle quayside. The Constructor eventually left the Pickfords fleet in December 1967, then went to Northern Ireland Carriers to perform more sterling heavy haulage work.

With Pickfords buying so many Constructors, it became difficult to tell them apart, but in the case of companies like Siddle Cook, of Consett, who bought only one of the big 6x6s, their machines were far more identifiable. SPT 600 was driver Walter Tomlinson's regular machine, and was seen in the Sherburn Terrace depot by the author in May 1962. The oddly placed mirror on the large radiator was mainly to ensure that no-one was standing in the blind spot when the vehicle was about to be moved but also to assist when coupling up the front drawbar pin. In mid-1986, SPT 600 was still in one piece, being located on the forecourt of a Datsun dealer in Glastonbury, awaiting a prospective purchaser from Northern Ireland.

Sunter Bros, of Northallerton, were also to buy a 6x6 Constructor. One of the many claims to fame of NAJ 920 was that it was road tested by *Commercial Motor* magazine prior to delivery in 1955. Although many exalted heavy haulage drivers would decry the driving technique exhibited by Alan Williams, of Scammell, in this excellent *Commercial Motor* photograph, the manoeuvre does show the design and flexibility of the cross-articulating front suspension, which had been a Scammell trademark since 1927. The magazine recorded that the Constructor weighed 12.75 tons, and 11.5 tons of ballast weight were then carried by the tractor which had a wheelbase of 16ft and an overall length close to 25ft.

Due to the small size of the standard Constructor cab, very few of that type were to be found used on UK heavy haulage work. One notable exception was 358 ETN, which performed sterling work for Hill of Botley. As the TN part of the registration denotes, the Scammell originally started work in Northumbria, as a drilling rig carrier. The Hill solution to the limited accommodation was to build large crew quarters behind the original cab, the extra-long wheelbase permitting this type of construction. Seen manoeuvring at Portslade Power Station, near Brighton, on March 25, 1966, driver Ron Allen is being directed by John Farrington as they collect an 80-ton stator due to be taken for repair on board the 100-ton hydraulically suspended Crane girder trailer. Twenty years on, Chris Hill, seen here standing beside the waiting Mountaineer, was running the family heavy haulage business, while the 6x6 Scammell was still in one piece at the company's depot, but fighting a losing battle with the invading blackberry bushes.

44

The new range of Scammells arrived in the nick of time, for the weights that heavy hauliers were expected to move had been dramatically on the increase. This C.A. Parsons transformer weighed 165 tons which at the time made it the heaviest transformer to be moved by road in Britain. PUC 471 is making this acute turn at South Gosforth, just north of Newcastle, on its way to Blyth Power Station on September 13, 1956. Even though the outfit had two more Constructors pushing at the rear, with the trailer turning in this manner they could offer very little help to the leading tractor. Effectively, therefore, at this point it was moving close to 280 tons all on its own, which is well beyond anything Scammell originally envisaged for the standard Constructor.

Above: PUC 472 is seen heading up a similar roadtrain, this time on December 11, 1956, again carrying a C.A. Parsons transformer. It is a measure of the inadequacies of the UK road network at that time that this relatively small transformer, built in Newcastle, had to be shipped to Liverpool prior to the six-day road haul to Ferrybridge, which is almost as close to the Tyneside starting point as it is to Merseyside. PUC 472, chassis number 8995, went off the Pickfords fleet in December 1967 and, like PUC 474, was to end up with Hill of Botley. Also to be found later in the Southampton area was this Crane 200-ton capacity trailer, which at the time of writing is in the North Baddesley yard of Shamara Heavy Haulage, still fit for work. Opposite: although the electrical industry was the source of most heavy traffic for Pickfords' Scammells, the company's expertise was often requested in other areas of industry too. This Appleby Frodingham Steel Company photograph shows the Birtley-based Crane Fruehauf trailer T1104 in Crosby Warren Quarry, near Scunthorpe, on October 19, 1965. Driver Alan Hutchinson, trailerman Bill Napier and the other Pickfords staff are involved in the short haul of a fully rigged 110 RB machine. The 175-ton capacity, eight-axled load carrier, which was later to be sold abroad, utilized its hydraulic suspension to raise and lower its charge. However, the crew are here building up a timber roadway so that when they dropped the 110 tons of weight they would still have room underneath to remove the frame girders.

47

The Mountaineer was an obvious smaller alternative to the big Constructor, and this ICI photograph, taken in July 1956, shows MUL 249 having just finished a short haul from the South Durham Iron and Steel works at Stockton to Billingham. There were 35 tons in this 90ft long, 10ft diameter column, supported on the 30-ton capacity Crane bogies which, due to their compact size and strength, are still in demand today by the enterprising heavy haulier. The Scammell was based at Birmingham, which at the time was one of Pickfords' leading heavy haulage depots in the country.

298 FUW was an even smaller-wheelbase version of the Mountaineer. Although this Scammell originally started life with the Royal Air Force, it was with Hill of Botley that it worked its hardest. The haulier modified it into ballast box form from its original articulated version. The Hill crew are seen in mid-1966 at Boldre Wood, in the New Forest, where the load consists of about 30 tons of 98ft long radar masts intended for the RAF, but destined first to go to Burt Bolton's timber yard for treatment. The rearmost steerable bogie is quite special, being a product of Bridge Commercials, a Hill-owned engineering offshoot.

TGJ 681 was always referred to as Billy Sinclair's wagon by the staff of the Pickfords Birtley depot. Chassis number 9602 first went to work in December 1956 and is seen here far from home, trying to squeeze through Brecon on its way to Neath with a machine component supported on the Crane frame trailer. In this situation, the Constructor could be a big, unwieldy beast, and unfortunately a shop window came off worst following an argument with the outfit, even though the policeman at the driver's window is doing his best to help.

Opposite: the 6x4 Junior Constructor bridged the gap between the four-wheeled Mountaineer and the larger 6x6 Constructor. UXC 617 was one of a batch of 20 similar Scammells put on the road by Pickfords in the period from November 1957 to January 1958. M1831 was disposed of in March 1968, and throughout its life the coachbuilt mudwings were invariably in need of minor repair, due to the rigorous demands of heavy haulage work. The outfit is pictured here outside Foster, Yates and Thom Ltd, of Blackburn, the 61-ton boiler, with a running height of 16ft, being an ideal fit for the standard 60-ton Crane float. Above: XUC 855 is an example showing the different type of front mudguards used on the Scammell range at this time, these being known as cycle wings. Chassis number 10690 was built during late 1960, and went first to the construction company of Wimpey. Sunters were to buy the Junior Constructor around 1965, and driver Bill Jemison is seen in this British Steel photograph on a relatively short haul from Teeside Bridge & Engineering to the Lackenby Basic Oxygen Steel (BOS) plant on February 19, 1970. The 250-ton casting ladle was in essence a massive bowl, where the assorted ingredients to make steel were mixed together. Taps at the bottom allowed the molten metal to pour first into a pair of tundishes and then to either a continuous casting system to make slabs or blooms, or alternatively into moulds to make ingots.

874 AUU was bought new by Marples, Ridgeway & Partners Ltd, who were the contractors for the construction of the Hammersmith flyover in London. Together with a Crane float drawbar trailer, the Scammell was involved in the movement of the heavy pre-cast units which were joined together on site. There were 204 beam segments, which formed the main spine beam throughout the structure and weighed up to 60 tons each; 204 cantilever units, which supported the outer lanes of the roadways and weighed approximately 15 tons each; and 408 road slabs. All these units, which in total weighed 14,000 tons, were hauled by the Leyland 680-powered Junior Constructor over a distance of about 9 miles. Once the job was finished, the outfit was sold to Jack Hill, at Botley, and it is seen above left, still in its original owner's basic colours, negotiating the Milbrook roundabout. The 28-ton, 20ft-high propeller was destined for the passenger liner *Canberra*, and travelled between Southampton docks and South London. Hill soon modified the Junior for more all-round work and she is seen above right in early 1974 in articulated form supporting a 60-ton piling machine to be used in the early construction of the M27 motorway at Swanwick.

Left: Chris Miller also made use of the Junior Constructor in articulated form, HJA 148F being bought at an auction in Leeds. It was originally coupled to a four-in-line Crane semi-trailer, although it is seen here hauling Dyson running gear that started life in a semi-trailer owned by British Nuclear Fuels Ltd. One of the jobs the Junior performed was to haul the dismembered parts of Oakenclough Paper Mill from Garstang to Preston Docks, in 1975, *en route* to Africa. The mill's new owner also asked Chris Miller if he would sell HJA 148F, and as the price was right the Junior became another Scammell export success.

HPY 54D, chassis number 20805, was Sunters' third and final Junior Constructor, being first registered in July 1966. The vehicle's first driver was Jimmy Goulding, and the 680-powered Scammell is seen just outside Bristol in January 1967. This imported column came in via Avonmouth Docks, and although the 85-ton weight and 110ft length were not excessive, the height limitation inside the ICI factory where it was delivered provided a headache.

Wynns may not have operated as many Scammells as Pickfords during the 1950s, but this did not reflect on how competitive they were with the Ninth Division of British Road Services. Although Pickfords had up to 26 depots spread throughout the country, when it came to heavy haulage in Wales, and particularly South Wales, Wynns were very keen to show that anything those blue vehicles with the lion on the door could do, they could do as well, if not better. The classic move by Wynns seen on these pages may feature only one Scammell, slightly overawed by the line-up ahead of it, a Ward Le France wrecker, a Foden 100-tonner and two Pacifics, but this should not detract from the contribution it made to the haul. Wynns were able to move the Ransome Rapier No 4140 Electric Excavator, weight 146 tons in this fully rigged condition, between two mountain top quarries in South Wales so that their customer was able to continue operations with the loss of only one weekend. HDW 519, the rearmost tractor, was rated as a 25-tonner; it was new to Wynns in 1951 and was given the fleet number 213.

Left: although the Junior Constructor was introduced in 1956, it was not until 10 years later that Siddle Cook were to buy their first example, and by this time the previously family-owned firm had been sold out to the Tay-Forth Group. Geoff Cook continued to run the Consett operations and, like his father, he endeavoured to keep up a family tradition whereby all the home-registered vehicles had their numbers ending in 00. This Arthur Philipson photograph, taken in 1967, shows the Leyland-powered Scammell with an awkward fabrication resting on Crane bogies on an internal move within the Consett Iron Company works.

Left: once the coachbuilt cab was modified to fit the Junior Constructor, it was also offered on the 4x4 Mountaineer. Wynns, of Newport, did not take to anything in the Constructor range, but they utilized a lot of the smaller 20-tonners in the 1950s and 1960s. This Mountaineer was one of two put into service during 1956-57 and, as the badge on the radiator denotes, it was Meadows-powered. Seen by the author in about 1962, it is outside Kellys Cafe, at Boroughbridge, trailing part of a major export success; Metropolitan-Vickers were to supply South African Railways with 135 locomotives, which were shipped out via Liverpool Docks.

Right: outwardly, the Super Constructor did not look a great deal different from the Constructor range it complemented. The obvious change visible in this Australian photograph is the modified front suspension. In place of the rocking front axle on a centrally pivoting transverse spring is a similar rocking beam, but with the road shocks absorbed by helical coil springs. The tractor unit of this oilfields artic is a load carrier in its own right, as the fifth-wheel coupling is sunk into the steel deck, thus not obstructing general use of the platform. Very few of these 35ft long, 10ft wide semi-trailers were used in the UK, due to legal difficulties, but those that were could carry 50 to 60 tons of payload with little difficulty.

WYH 901 (opposite) and WYH 902 (above) which had chassis numbers 10431 and 10432, were two of the earliest Super Constructors put to work by Pickfords in March 1960. They had a softer line to their crew cab than the gaunt expression of the Constructor, and both these Leyland/Albion 900-powered Scammells were left-hand drive. The arguments for and against where the steering wheel should be placed could be won for either side, but Pickfords felt that as the big machines rarely wanted to overtake anyone, gaining better vision of the nearside kerb was of far more importance. George Godden is at the helm of M2211 as he prepares for the harrowing descent to Rugeley Power Station, not long after the vehicle was put into service. M2212 is seen in about 1966 coupled to the easily identifiable Scammell semi-trailer with dolly, which was built in 1929 to be coupled to the original 100-tonner artic. LMS locomotive 6233 was named *Duchess of Sutherland*.

Above: Sunter Bros were to run two Super Constructors, KVN 860E being chassis number 20897, put into service in July 1967. This Dennis Wompra photograph, taken on July 17, 1967, shows driver John Robinson clarifying the route to be taken with these two awkward fabrications from Yarm Road, Stockton, to Middlesbrough Docks. They were part of a complete Kaldo plant built by Whessoe and destined for British Steel at South Wales, the motor vessel *Con Brio* doing the nautical leg of the journey. The Scammell is hauling eight rows of Scheuerle running gear, while the following Rotinoff is hauling its load on the Crane solid bogies. Sunters' other Super Constructor, chassis number 15235, was registered 447 DPY and was to end up with Smith Bros, of Waterloo Mills, Pudsey, doing recovery work. Opposite: using the semi-automatic transmission of the Super Constructor, Scammell produced a batch of four-wheeled tractor units for Pickfords, rated for about 65 tons gross operation. M3022 was based at Birmingham/Walsall, although trailer TM818, a 90-ton capacity Crane, plus pushing Constructor PUC 472 were both on loan from Birtley for the haul of this GEC transformer to La Collette Power Station, in Jersey, during November 1965. John Marshall, from that North East depot, had done a great deal of research to find a suitable route to the Channel Islands destination preparatory to C.A. Parsons, of Tyneside, winning the relevant orders for equipment, although he was not allowed to go there for a working holiday! In the end, GEC made the cargo and the Birmingham depot managed the haul. With modern-day ro-ro ships still in the planning stage, Pickfords had to use an army landing craft to do the sea crossing as the conventional ferry ramp would not give the clearance needed for the girder trailer.

3: CONTRACTORS IN DEMAND

Just as the Constructor had upstaged the Pioneer, the arrival of the Contractor, in 1964, represented an entirely new range of vehicles from Scammell. Whilst the all-wheel-drive 6x6 Constructor certainly had its advantages, the first immediate difference in the new product was that it was of 6x4 configuration, without that driven front axle. As there would always be a certain demand for all-wheel-drive six-wheeled vehicles, production of the Super Constructor was continued while the new range attracted a wider band of users.

In keeping with the trend of the fashionable 1960s, Scammell abandoned the gaunt lines of the Constructor and adopted a smoother style for the Contractor which was more pleasing to the eye. The basic cab was again a type of hand-me-down, being a variation on the well-known LAD (Leyland-Albion-Dodge) product made from pressed steel. Although Albion and Dodge continued to make use of this accommodation, Leyland/AEC were more interested in promoting their longer-lived Ergomatic cab, which first saw life in 1963. One thing unchanged from the Constructor range, however, was the chassis, which was of pressed-steel, bolted construction, being over 12 inches deep and ½ inch thick.

To decide on a suitable power source, Scammell were in a far better position than they had been 10 years earlier. Cummins, the American manufacturer, had come to Britain in 1956, and their presence had been a major influence in truck operations since then. The Rolls-Royce 12.17-litre engine, now called the Eagle and developing 300bhp, was still favoured as the first option by many operators, although the Cummins NT335 or the even more powerful NT380 mainly found favour with the power-seeking heavy hauliers.

The Scammell gearbox did not survive the transition from Constructor to Contractor and a 15-speed Fuller was supplied instead when a manual gear-change was specified. The alternative when far heavier weights were to be hauled was a straight descendant from the Super Constructor, namely the Self Changing Gears RV30 eight-speed semi-automatic box. An additional option to this latter transmission was a two-speed epicyclic splitter, which had the effect of offering a total of 15 very closely spaced forward ratios, augmented by two in reverse. Unlike the usual splitter shift-lever, which is normally mounted in close proximity on the hand gear-lever, the Scammell splitter was operated by a large flap-type pedal strategically placed on the floor, where a conventional clutch pedal would normally have been found had it not been removed when the semi-auto box was fitted.

Engine and gearbox apart, the area where the Contractor reflected its true strength was in its back end, with a bogie offered in three options up to an incredible 40 tons capacity. The standard suspension on the heavyweight range might have seemed slightly conventional in the use of leaf springs, but being mounted centrally and upside-down (inverted), their massive size, linked to enormous hubs which incorporated epicyclic reduction gearing, gave away the true potential of the tractor.

In typical Scammell style, the strongest Contractor was rated to perform at a mere 240 tons train weight. When you bear in mind that these ballasted tractors were to tip the scales at anything between 40 and 50 tons, hauling a 12-axle girder trailer that weighed just over 100 tons unladen meant that there was only room for a payload of 100 tons in Scammell's eyes, theoretically the same as with those pacesetting terrible twins built 35 years earlier. Protestations wouldn't move Scammell from their calculated maximum, but what the Contractor proved capable of doing in practice made some at Watford simply shudder in fear, whilst it made others on the factory floor push their chests out with pride at what a machine they had built.

Bearing witness to this, I once saw Peter Clemmett and his *Fearnought* perform a move on a wet and miserable winter's day in Whessoe's Dockpoint yard on Teesside. There was a weight of over 1,100 tonnes in a module that was to be pushed backwards by two Contractors, a Titan and a Tractomas. Peter was slightly too keen to get on with it and started ahead of the others, pushing the module and pulling the other three tractors at the same time before wheelspin let him down on the greasy concrete apron.

Payloads reckoned in thousands of tons may not have been even a daydream in the mid-1960s, but loads in excess of 300 tons were a frightening reality as early as 1967. Pickfords were to meet the challenge of moving such weights by buying large numbers of Contractors, the first 240-tonner being NYE 593E. All of these vehicles, whether rated at 125 or 240 tons, were to have the large four-door crew cab, which in essence was a rounded-off version of the type fitted to their small batch of Super Constructors.

Robert Wynn & Sons, based in Newport, were also to buy the large crew-cabbed versions, but they soon put to work the basic-cab Contractors to replace their ageing Diamond Ts, which had been recabbed and re-engined to keep them at work. Wynns worked these ex-American tank transporters hard, although one trick used by their drivers could not be found in the vehicle's handbook. Traction was always a problem with heavy haulage, for if you lose it on a gradient and the outfit starts to slide then it is a case of fingers crossed and let destiny take charge of the situation. Bearing this in mind, the Wynns crew simply used their own on-board power winch. Running the cable out, it was fixed to somewhere strategic on the heavily loaded drawbar trailer. Then, by tightening the winch cable, the tractor was pulled downwards even harder on to the road surface.

Manufacturers of modern conventional 38-tonners may pull faces at such a trick, even though their method of dumping the air from an axle's suspension in order to transfer the weight and overload the tractor's drive axle to aid traction is simply a variation on this theme of physics. The Diamond T may have got through its fair share of transmission half-shafts by rebelling at acts like this, but their drivers and mates became experts at being able to fish out the broken pieces and replace them with a new shaft with practised ease.

Whether with a small or large cab, the Contractor immediately became the recognized leader in the heavy-haulage tractor stakes. It seemed as though anyone who wanted to be recognized as a heavy haulier of repute bought one of the big Scammells, but even though the Watford marque was close to being unchallenged in the UK in the late 1960s and early 1970s, the Contractor had to make its presence felt in the export market to retain that high standing and leadership.

Jordan was to buy the new Scammell for a variety of roles, and whilst ICI were to use the Contractor up to 85 tons as an artic dumper in Great Britain, its Australian roadtrain counterpart had to run at 160 tons gross with anything up to three dangling trailers running behind it. Logging Contractors went to work in the forests of Ghana and New Zealand, whilst Dale Freightways, the largest heavy haulier in the latter country, understandably chose the Contractor for their outsize traffic. In South Africa it was Thorntons who were the leaders in that type of haulage, and although they used some strange Foden ballasted tractor eight-wheelers as hauling locomotives, the big Contractors were soon incorporated into their fleet.

Thornton Transportation had been founded in 1892, and in

1962 they were taken over by the United Group of Companies who, two years later, bought out the respected family concerns of Wynns and Sunters in the UK. Thorntons, like every other haulier in Southern Africa, were fighting against the commanding position that South African Railways were able to hold over the entire area of goods transportation. But with the start of big chemical plants like Sasol (oil from coal), Thorntons were quickly after the out-of-gauge traffic that could not be hauled by rail.

Being part of the United Group meant there was a limited interchange of staff between the UK and Africa, and as well as importing British Contractors, Thorntons management was keen to attract practical experts to show them how to physically transport the virtually impossible. Bill Langham was one of the Pickfords Birmingham-based staff who moved to the other side of the equator, and he tells one story that reflects how arduous working conditions are in Africa.

Bill was driving a lead tractor up towards the Kariba Dam one day, a project which created a great deal of local interest whenever a big load went past. To ease the discomfort of the searing sun in the hot cab, Bill had taken off his shirt and loosened the waistband of his trousers. Prior to the tricky descent to the site itself Bill decided to leap out of the cab and check over the rig — the crowd of watching females finding it a far more interesting sight when his trousers fell off.

The first Contractors ran by Thorntons were standard-cab versions, which ran either as artics or in ballasted form. Later ones, however, were built with locally constructed Sautini cabs, which resembled the glassfibre units used on early 1960s Guy Invincibles.

Phillip Morris-Jones bought two of these Sautini versions from Thorntons when he was setting up his heavy haulage business in Germiston. One passed its best was cut down to form a substantial bogie, whilst the other unfortunately was to meet a tragic demise by sliding down a large ravine just outside Cape Town. The reason for the accident was put down to a mixture of thick fog and black ice, although some superstitious people felt that the Scammell had been doomed once it had received its fateful fleet number of 13, a mistake Phillip says he would never repeat in his current Red House Motor Services fleet.

Ravines apart, these early Contractors worked well in Africa. There are not many countries where you can travel from sea-level to 6,000 feet, encountering temperatures from freezing point to 120 degrees Fahrenheit all in the same day, and where your hauls might stretch to anything up to 1,000 miles in distance. The men from Wynns all have memories of Africa as most of the fleet's big Contractors were to work on the sub-continent at some time in their life, some of them never to return from their final resting places in Sudan.

In traditional railway locomotive fashion, John Wynn had carried on the habit of individually naming his heavyweight haulers. The Contractors had emotive titles like *Conqueror, Challenger, Crusader, Hercules, Champion, Resolute* and *Talisman*. Strong, grand sounding names they may be, and if looks could count for anything then the Contractor just oozed with confidence, but when it came to actually driving the machine, chauffeurs like Bill Jemison would certainly have a go at the Pride of Watford.

Bill reckoned that the steering was far too fussy, always requiring a slight correction, a problem never encountered with the all-wheel-drive Super Constructor. The power assistance may have been quite reasonable with the big Cummins working hard, but once those revs died down you needed a lot of Northallerton brawn to pull that wheel around.

As far as driver comforts were concerned, the Contractor offered very few. The driving seat was totally uncompromising and the double passenger seat in the big crew cab was mounted too far forward. Replaced 6 inches further back, it then allowed the driver to see out of the nearside mirror, although rearward vision past the full-width ballast box was extremely limited. Bill recalls nearly pushing down Sunter's main garage when he lost its main supporting post in the tractor's massive blind spot.

The Contractor cab is large and airy, although trying to read a newspaper under the illumination of the glow-worm-type interior light is close to impossible. Cleaning the outside windows requires the use of extendable arms if you don't want to climb on top of the rounded bonnet, for the size of the

The Contractor range was announced in 1964, the smooth lines of the new Scammell flagship bringing the Watford vehicles into line with the fashionable 1960s. It was offered as a general haulage vehicle, but the strong Scammell pedigree meant that not many Contractors were to be run at the nominal maximum weight, which at the time was only 24 tons for articulated vehicles. This Dyson Trailers photograph shows one of three articulated tippers that were supplied to Ali-Bin-Ali, Doha, Qatar in 1977, offering a payload potential of 50 tons. These Contractors had chassis numbers WHV 4547-8-9.

windscreen washer bottles seems strangely small. Whilst there may be some of us who simply sigh at the sight of a Contractor, when you live day in and day out around one, the gentle giant shows its rough spots.

Bill had driven most types of Scammell of the era, but his love for the open road blended strangely with a great deal of time spent as a drag line operator on open cast coal sites. They didn't look anything like heavy haulage tractors, but the type of transmission used in some of the large site dumpers seemed to have something special about them. So when Peter Sunter was deciding to invest in three more of the big 240-tonners, Bill suggested that the V16 Detroit mated to an Allison gearbox and torque converter might be a big improvement on the Cummins-RV30 combination. The later story of having to use a Land-Rover to help Bill pull over 200 tons up a steep hill was a suggestion of how right he was, but it was only Peter Searson and his hybrid conversions of the Contractors into Heanor Haulage Tractors who seemed to be on the same wavelength so far as it related to the Detroit power pack. History records that the Jemison suggestion did not bear fruit, not at that time.

The first 240-ton Contractor to be bought by Pickfords was chassis number 20918, being one of a pair, the consecutive registrations being NYE 593E and 594E. They were put into service in April 1967 and Pickfords tended to work them together in pull-push combination, having the 12-axle 300-ton girder trailer TM 1277 wedged between them. But there were only 210 tons in this Parsons Peebles transformer, which was one of three built in Edinburgh and destined for the Vales Point power house, New South Wales, Australia. Pickfords were to drive them onto the Starman boat, where the rigging crew were to self-unload them, but they were craned off at the Australian Naval Dockyard, Garden Island, before Fleetexpress finished the haul, again with a type of girder trailer, but this time headed up by a brace of Mack Tractor units.

Scammell set their eyes on satisfying the foreign market for tank transporters, even though the British Army had consolidated on the Thornycroft Antar. Their military Contractor, like the one seen on demonstration above, was specifically built to carry 55 tons of payload at speeds up to 46mph with a gradient ability of more than 15%. The Cummins 335bhp engine was the standard fitment, with a cooling system that had been successfully operated at 48 degrees C. The standard winch fitted to this Contractor, mounted behind the cab, was equipped with 430ft of rope.

Wynns quickly opted for the standard-cabbed Contractor as a replacement for their maturing Diamond Ts, GDW 231D being registered in April 1965, when it was given the fleet number 189. It is seen, left, manoeuvring what was termed an excessively large pallet onto an Atlantic Container Lines ship at Liverpool Docks. The Wynns three-line bogies had picked this up end-suspension wise, which in essence meant that a load-carrying trailer was not unnecessarily hauled to the United States. On dry land the quartet of Contractors may still have been hauling tank-transporting trailers, but they could give a better spread of performance than the superseded Diamond T. The line of vehicles in well marshalled convoy, right, are carrying Marston-Excelsior heat exchangers, which were approximately 18ft wide and weighed 45 tons, from Wolverhampton.

An outfit which encompassed the involvement of Scammell, Crane Fruehauf, Head Wrightson (Teesdale) Ltd, the Niger Dam Authority, Wynns and Sunters was called by Head Wrightson the Rolls-Royce road-rail wagon, but was also known to Jon Lauder and other Wynns personnel as *The Yellow Peril*. The Alan Simpson photograph opposite shows the outfit leaving Head Wrightson's works into Mandale Road, Thornaby, on July 12, 1967. Heads had built the girders and interchangeable rail bogies because access to Onitsha, in Nigeria, was particularly difficult and required both modes of transport. The Niger Dam Authority photograph above, taken on November 24, 1972, shows the outfit on the Onitsha wharf, where the transformer load is being carried inside the girder frame rather than sitting on it. The shirtless runner is Barry Setterfield, although Wynns encouraged local staff and in the main acted only as supervisors. The second Contractor had the local registration LN 8144.

Chassis number WHV 4023 started life in February 1968, painted in the bright red livery of Siddle Cook and registered XUP 999F. John Black managed to salvage this Arthur Philipson photograph after heavy haulage operations were closed at Consett about 1973. Regular driver Walter Tomlinson is pictured on June 3, 1970 taking this newly constructed coke car on Crane bogies from Consett Iron Company's main works on a short haul to the Fell Coke Works. The Contractor was later to be given the Pickfords fleet number M8542, and, after changing hands several times, in 1983 it was bought by Shamara Heavy Haulage, of North Baddesley, near Southampton, and put back to work in a blue-and-white colour scheme.

In contrast to the single crew-cab 240-ton Contractor bought by Cook in 1968, by that time Pickfords already had three separate batches on the road. The first, NYE 593E and 594E of April 1967, had been followed by PGO 711E, 712E and 713E of June/July 1967. The next large batch of six had registration letters SYO, with 400F, the last in that line, going into service in January 1968. The gleaming Contractor is seen in mid-1968 leaving Foster Wheeler, at Hartlepool, hauling the well-travelled TM818 Crane frame trailer. The Scammell is not over-burdened in weight for this haul, but particularly noteworthy is how the package boiler is being carried inside the frame, end-suspensionwise, to keep the running height down to a minimum.

The Contractor was amenable to heavy haulage operations either as a ballasted tractor or as a tremendously strong articulated tractor unit. Not a great deal of weight for *Enterprise*, left, as it threads its way through Eccleshall, Staffordshire, with this boat which had been built at Stone. Ken Johnson is one of the performers of the wire act, regular drivers of this left-hand-drive Scammell being Dennis Carpenter and Gerry Guard. The Scheuerle 80-ton capacity trailer was of girder construction, which allowed the keel of this boat to sit partially in the open space. With the Scheuerle disposed of, Wynns were to utilize the same girders in King semi-trailer number 1032, which was seen by Peter Lee travelling south down the M5 at Strensham in mid-1979, right. Of special note is the trailer bogie with automatic steering through the two main axles and a third tag one.

Although all of Pickfords' Contractors were to be fitted with the identical looking crew cab, a comparison of M5034, headed up by M5297, above, easily shows the difference between the 240-tonner and its smaller 125-ton counterpart. Although the ballast body has a slightly different line, it is the massive tyre equipment and the size of the rear wheel hubs which really reflect the strength of the heavyweight. WGC 637G had chassis number WHV 4101 and came into service in September 1968, while SYO 384F had chassis number 21546, being new to Pickfords in November 1967. The duo are seen surmounting Byker Bank *en route* to North Shields with this 125-ton NEI Parsons stator outer casing supported on the newly acquired eight rows of Nicolas modular running gear.

Stanlow, in 1971, was one of the turning points for the heavy haulage industry in that it reflected just how nearly limitless the ability of the expert mover could be. Wynns knew that this job would not be without its problems and its drama, for pioneering work is always a matter of stepping out into the unknown and seeing what happens. Grabbing the limelight here were the Wynns Contractors, with *Conqueror*, fleet number 182, registration NDW 836G, hauling the largest of the three massive loads, one which was 28ft in diameter, 111ft long and 212 tonnes in weight. This Shell photograph, taken on December 19, recalls the measured progress along the A41 road near Hooton, and the fascination of the local population in such a gigantic task.

Just as the late 1950s saw massive purchases by Pickfords of the Junior Constructor range, 10 years on Pickfords were to place similar large orders for the smaller-weight Contractor range. WYO 295H was one of the last batch of 11 Scammells classified by Pickfords as 100-tonners. It had chassis number WHV 4270 and was put into service in April 1970. The Contractor is hauling Crane girder trailer fleet number 666, which was based at Liverpool and is seen here supporting a paper reel as it leaves Darwen Paper Mill for Liverpool Docks. The load is supported on a specially placed skid, both to protect the fine finish machined onto the reel and to support it on its lengthy sea journey.

Sunters' first 240-tonner was registered TPY 675H, being chassis number WHV 4312, and it went into service during June 1970. It is probably best remembered for its dual identity, for after a rebuild it was re-registered YVN 308T. An early job for the new Scammell involved the haul of this dock gate destined for Workington Docks. The gate had been assembled in the dock area from parts road-hauled across the Pennines from Teesside. John Robinson, driving the Contractor, is easing down the specially laid roadway with the gate supported on the ex-Wynns Scheuerle trailer. The gate was then lowered onto specially positioned stools near the water's edge and, when the tide came in, it floated off and was pulled into position inside the docks by a sea-going tug. During the mid-1980s, this and three similar Scammells were sold to India.

Described as a desalter and designed to extract salt from sea water by a chemical process, this 110-ton vessel was one of about 13 similar constructions built by Danks of Netherton and destined for the Gulf States via Liverpool Docks. UDW 139J was new to Wynns in 1971, and is seen just outside Netherton works, at Dudley, about 1975. The Nicolas three-line bogies have been deliberately adjusted to adopt this strange deflection so that as the load negotiated a sharp hump-back bridge, the bogies' movement would ensure that the load remained level. The limitations of the ballast box capacity are also illustrated on this Scammell, which was to be shipped out by Wynns for use on their Nigerian contract in 1978.

LFB 716K, opposite, was another Scammell which was to do a great deal of work in distant climes, but initially it was bought by Sparrows to move what was described at the time as the largest mobile crane in the world, over 500ft in height and with a capacity for 500 tons of lift. The 240-ton rated tractor, fitted with the Cummins NTK 335 engine, was not overworked by Sparrows, who were to sell it on to Watkinsons, the general/heavy haulier of Keighley. It did not end its crane work, however, for Watkinsons were the main mover for all the girders built by crane manufacturers John Smith. Driver Michael Albone is pushing one of Smith's longest productions into this Tor Line vessel, above, at Immingham during 1982, for delivery by Watkinsons to a steel works just outside Oslo. This Contractor is recalled as being a bit of a rogue, and it was sold on to Whessoe, who took it out to Sri Lanka, where Sunter drivers like Jimmy Goulding used it to push pipes down mountain sides; Whessoe were involved in a scheme there similar to their work for the pumped storage station at Dinorwic, North Wales.

Being the largest heavy haulier in Southern Africa, Thorntons naturally took to the new Contractor range fairly soon after it was announced. This Phillip Morris-Jones photograph, taken in 1968, shows two of Watford's best engaged in the 20-mile haul of an 80-ton bridge beam from Johannesburg. With nearby Rhodesia being particularly strong on weight checks and axle loadings, Thorntons were keen to ensure ample wheels under their load and this small semi-trailer/dolly was made in South Africa by Jack Plane. The pushing Contractor, albeit having the look of a bonneted ERF built for export, is in fact fitted with a cab built locally by Sautini.

Exporting Contractors as far afield as Australia, Scammell normally shipped them in a fashion termed CKD (Completely Knocked Down). They were assembled on the other side of the world, and, understandably, local builders were keen to stamp their own trademark on the finished product. Watford were never to feature an eight-wheeled Contractor in their own specification brochures, but this example, with a second steering axle added on for a discerning customer, would naturally meet approval from the men on the factory floor, who thrive on ingenuity.

Wrekin Roadways always favoured the Scammell product, but it was not until 1975 that they bought their first crew-cabbed 240-ton Contractor, chassis number WHV 4514, which was registered JNT 522N. Driver Bill Lewis is seen in this Poclain photograph having just left the Seaforth terminal, at Liverpool, for a relatively short haul to Wigan, the 15ft wide load being well supported on the popular Crane Fruehauf girder trailer. Robert James, now a director of Wrekin Transport Services, recalls that due to Bill Lewis' fine driving technique, this Contractor cost his old company next to nothing in maintenance charges prior to the merger with Wynns. In December 1984, the Scammell was drained of water, a victim of the recession in heavy haulage, and six months later it was refurbished at Northallerton and sold to a customer in India.

Left: a regular destination for Wynns' Contractors was the so-called Knuckle at Pomona Dock, in Manchester. This term was used to distinguish the area where the heavy-lift ships were tied up. *Resolute* is seen in about 1976 unloading a 265-ton inner stator from GEC Stafford ready for export on a ship of the Mammoet fleet. The girder trailer being used on this occasion is the 14-line Nicolas, which had fleet number 987.

Right: although the Contractor range is renowned for its sheer pulling strength, the shrewd heavy haulier will tell you that a reliable winch in good hands is worth its weight in gold. This Norman Macleod photograph, taken in September 1973, illustrates how Pickfords co-ordinated the use of two winching Scammells to side-haul a 243-ton Ferranti transformer into the Foyers generating station, on the side of Loch Ness. Restrictive road structure in the area prevented access to a conventional girder trailer or heavy lift cranes, and Pickfords were to simply winch the transformer into position inside the station using the Contractors and small skate-type wheels known as doddlers. The tractors involved were M6203 and M6204, chassis numbers WHV 4260 and 4262, both 100-tonners, put into service in February and May 1970, respectively.

Left: the original shell of the standard cab fitted to the Contractor dated from the early 1960s, so it was obvious that Scammell would consider alternatives to bring the vehicle up to date. This Motor Panels cab is recognizable as the type used on the Crusader but, although some time has been spent on this mock-up, thankfully the concept never caught on. One operator who conducted a similar transplant was Tony Morgan, of Bridgend, who put a Marathon cab onto one of his Contractors, although the vehicle was sold to the Middle East before it was put to work. More pleasing on the eye was the Volvo F89 cab fitted by Peter Searson to his Scammell-HHTs.

Right: Dennis Roderick, driver for Wrekin Roadways, has moved a great deal of weight with his Scammell, but although there may have been only 35 tons in this ARC stone crusher, moving it up this loose gravel incline near Shrewsbury was particularly testing. The Scammell-headed Foden is negotiating a double-back turn close to the end of the haul. Of heavier weight was a Stanley Davies 80-ton mobile crane, which had to be double-headed to the top so that the stone crusher could be lifted off and placed in position. This Scammell had the Wrekin fleet number 33, then the Wynns Heavy Haulage number 127. At the time of writing it was being operated by Roger Harris, of Abnormal Load Engineering, Stafford.

With the North Sea oil boom, the Contractor found itself asked to move all sorts of shapes, sizes and weights. The actual distances hauled may not have been particularly far, but some of the dimensions involved were phenomenal. Driver Jimmy Goulding is seen at the helm of HVN 397N in this BP photograph, taken on April 4, 1979, as the Contractor prepares to haul a 60ft high prefabricated piperack built at Charlton Leslie's, on Tyneside, back onto dry land at Sullom Voe, in the Shetlands. Sunter fleet number 197 spent a great deal of time in the north of Scotland, but was then painted white for work in the Gulf States. Ten years after starting life with Sunters in April 1975, it was one of four tractors sold to a customer in India.

The Contractors of Econofreight became well used to the sight of this huge lifting frame, for they were involved in its movement on four separate occasions. The Tom Llewellyn photograph above shows UVN 44S and TRL 924H working under close co-ordination to move the 280-ton mass on two 10-row Nicolas trailers into storage at the old Laing yard at Graythorpe, on the side of the Tees Bay, during 1983. The frame was designed for a multitude of differing lifts of modules destined for the gas exploration field in Morecambe Bay. The Scammells were to be repainted in the livery of Econofreight Heavy Transport, but following the merger of Econofreight and United (Wynns/Sunters) in May 1986, the two small-cabbed Contractors were sold to a dealer in Ripley, Derbyshire.

SJD 801F was chassis number 22118 and started life with Pickfords in January 1968, being given the original fleet number M5234. Jack Hill was to buy the Contractor in January 1980 from dealer George Hardwick, and it was soon expected to live up to its 125-tons train weight rating. It is seen, right, on one of its first jobs for Hill at Southampton Docks, towing off from the ACL vessel the first of four 120-ton shunting locomotives imported by Foster Yeoman.

On the day that the Prince and Princess of Wales were being married in July 1981, it was also one of the finest hours for Scammell Contractor TRL 924H. Tom Llewellyn's photograph shows *Betsy* reflecting on the 476-ton SIF vessel that she had just hauled into Esso's Fawley refinery. If the 5-mile road move wasn't difficult enough with something 193ft long and 42ft high, the actual lift into position was to demonstate how exacting a feat cranemanship can be; it took 12 hours with the three cranes working together to stand the distillation column in the desired position.

The glasses and pipe behind the wheel of Contractor LAJ 798P are an immediate giveway to identify driver Bill Jemison, who spent most of his working days with this Scammell after it took to the road in October 1975. The combination are seen up at Grangemouth, in early 1978, pushing this 70ft high storage tank back onto the Motor Vessel *Starman Africa*. In total eight of these 100-ton tanks were moved to Sullom Voe, although the vessel only carried a maximum of three at any one time. Loading and unloading the masses was done by utilizing the in-built hydraulics on the Nicolas load carrier. Some 11 years on from their original coming together, the Scammell was sent to India and Bill Jemison was to be found driving a small four-wheeled bowser round RAF Leeming.

To many, the Contractor is a big, slow, cumbersome lump, to others it is solid, strong, dependable and completely trustworthy. No matter which way you look at it, the track record of this Scammell product shows that it has moved some colossal loads, such as this impressive one coming ashore at Coryton, in Essex. *Buccaneer* was allocated the number 128 in the Wynns Heavy Haulage fleet, although it was originally listed with Wrekin Roadways as number 37.

4: HIGHWAYMEN AND COMMANDERS

At the lighter end of their range, Scammells had seemed to change very little, outwardly at least, from those early versions first offered in 1922. The solid tyres and chain drive had gone, of course, and diesel engines — predominantly of Gardner, Meadows or Leyland manufacture — had replaced the Scammell petrol units, but this apart, the machine was still very much of a similar basic, sturdy design.

The driving position remained erect, with the large steering wheel in profile to the sky. The independently mounted gearbox was gear-stick-operated through an awesome steel gate, but although some drivers were to detest the 'no frills' approach of the truck, as far as the operators went, its ability to go on and on, taking all sorts of abuse, meant that the Scammell was a natural backbone to many fleets.

Once the canvas roof had been changed, even the shape of the cab had hardly been altered until the 1960s, when the swept round shape of the new Highwayman was offered to show that Scammell was capable of keeping up with the fashionable trend, if a little reluctantly. For general haulage purposes at that time, the Routeman eight-wheeler, Handyman and Trunker articulated units looked outstandingly different with their air-cooled type of plastic finned cab. To the robust heavy haulier these machines were untried and could well be a bit soft for their demanding line of work, so to meet demand the Highwayman stayed in production until 1970. Perhaps this staying power in the model is reflected in how Harrisons of

Sheffield still run Highwaymen up and down the M1 motorway on demanding general haulage work in the late 1980s.

The solitary complaint, if it could be termed that, which was regularly fired at the Scammell supertrucks was that they were perhaps far too strong. Any truck manufacturer is bound to build in a certain amount of tolerance to his product so that if it is rated to work at, for example, 38 tons train weight, it would in fact be safe to operate at around 50% above that mark without breaking the machine into pieces.

Scammell also followed this rule of thumb, but their safety margin was at times as high as 100% due to the workmanship and strength they built into their product. For example, the Contractor range was originally envisaged to be suitable for the weight range of 38 to 240 tons, but it was made so strong that many operators rarely considered it for work at the lower level.

As Scammell could not interest people in working a strong model which was down-rated, they decided to go for a lighter model that was up-rated, and in the late 1960s the Highwayman was eased into retirement with the appearance of the Crusader range. Originally it was a product jointly developed as a high-speed trunking vehicle for UK and continental work for the British Road Services division of the National Freight Corporation. But with another drive axle added, the 6x4 Crusader slotted into a gap that the ever-strengthening Contractor had appeared to create. The British army's Royal Engineers were to run this type of Crusader up to about 60 tons gross, while the Royal Corps of Transport put them to work at lighter weights, but at higher speeds.

The military versions of the Crusader were to have Leyland emblazoned on the front of them, and their standard engine fitment was the Rolls-Royce Eagle, now developing 305bhp and 856lb ft of torque and propelling the vehicle through 7.808:1 back axles. The gearbox was of Fuller make and offered a choice of 15 ratios, the top 10 being in a conventional range-change pattern. For heavier loads on more difficult terrain, a deep-reduction selection in the box via a separate toggle bar switch brought into play the five extra-low ratios that gave the Crusader the edge in offering its high spread of performance.

The export version, as well as many Crusaders put to work in the UK, came fitted with the General Motors V8 two-stroke engine which was normally referred to simply as the Detroit. Like the popular Foden and Commer two-stroke engines of the early 1960s, the Detroit two-stroke had a sound all of its own, and hearing that engine at work was simply music to anyone who appreciated the characteristic beat of the diesel engine.

This standard heavy-haulage Crusader was designed by the factory for operation at 65 tons train weight, but even though it was primarily a built-up four-wheeler, the safety margin built into the design by Scammell meant that Crusaders were run by some operators at 100 tons gross and above without any difficulty. This type of reliability endeared the 65-tonner to many users who were prepared to accept some of the failings of the truck, the most obvious of which being the old-fashioned non-tilt cab, which was not even available as a sleeper version until well into the 1970s.

The price tag of the Detroit-powered 65-ton Crusader in the 1977 listings was £24,000 — with an extra £1,164 for the sleeper cab option — which was not unreasonable bearing in mind its true ability. Wynns were one of the many operators who took to the Crusader, although at that time they were keen to see its capacity raised in an official manner. So, working in conjunction with the Welsh operator, Scammell strengthened it out, eased a lightweight Contractor bogie into the back end,

and rated it fit for 100 and possibly 110 tons train weight, still not as high as the 150 tons that Wynns were really looking for. Scammell simply called this version their 100-ton Crusader, although Wynns quickly replaced the badge, and by everyone else the design was known as the Amazon.

An even stronger name had been affixed to a very special Crusader built some seven years earlier, in 1970, but unfortunately the lone Samson was very much a one-off in UK operations, although six others were reportedly shipped out to Australia in knocked-down form.

Pickfords were to take delivery of this Samson after it had done the rounds of the commercial exhibitions in late 1970. Being an eight-wheeled tractive unit, the Samson, it was felt, would greatly enhance the appeal of the heavy-haulage articulated low-loader. The problem surrounding this outfit had always been that an excess amount of weight was imposed through the semi-trailer kingpin onto the drive axles of the tractive unit. Adding a second steering axle into a standard 13ft-wheelbase Crusader increased the tolerance and thus the potential for this Scammell, which was rated for 75 tons train weight operation.

That was the theory behind the production of the Samson, but all the publicity came to nought; there were simply no orders for it. The reason for this in hindsight is quite simple. Operators found that there was no need to buy the eight-wheeled Samson when a standard six-wheeled Crusader, although only officially rated at 65 tons, was quite capable of taking that extra 10 tons and more without any complaint. The Samson was simply made redundant, a victim of the high quality and good standing of its theoretically smaller brothers. Had the legislation been more in line with the practical operations of heavy haulage, then more fine looking eight-wheelers may have been seen, but as it was the concept simply became history.

Encouraging someone to buy what you have already produced may be difficult, and it can be a lot more interesting and attractive if someone asks you to make a truck to their design and then they follow through with a repeat order for another 124, especially when the price tag for each outfit is close to £250,000. Effectively, this is what happened in 1984, with the delivery of the first batch of Scammell Commander tank transporters to the British army as a replacement for the long-lived Thornycroft Antars.

The Antar had served the military well, but its basic design was over 30 years old and although army vehicles are not renowned for excessive mileage, especially during peacetime, the tank transporters were regular workers and replacement vehicles were long overdue. Naturally, with Thornycroft having disappeared into the Leyland/AEC empire, the army approached Scammell to see what they could come up with. The paperwork began to be exchanged in 1968 as the army listed their requirements from such a new vehicle. It was to be an exciting time for Scammell engineers like John Fadelle as, slowly, the endless meetings, discussions and mock-ups gradually evolved into a fascinating new machine.

The original feasibility study for producing such a machine had to consider new demands in performance, which had never previously been asked for from an outfit of this size. At first it was described as the 55-tonne transporter, as this was the weight of the Chieftain battle tank, the leading fighting implement then in service with the army. As its engine was to weigh in at 2 tonnes and the gearbox at 1¼ tonnes, it was decided fairly soon that both these items should be mounted separately for ease of installation and servicing.

Initially, a challenging design problem was the necessity to rear-mount the conventional cooling group behind the cab as the radiators required for a vehicle of this size were too large for mounting in the conventional position right at the front of the engine. However, subsequent advances in technology were to allow the production Commander to have its cooling system in the normal place.

The cooling trials themselves, intended to ascertain the maximum operating temperature, presented considerable technical problems in that a dynamometer load able to resist a tractive effort of 15 tonnes at 4.3 miles per hour had to be towed by the train in order to establish if the transmission was adequately cooled. This was achieved by towing three extra vehicles for a period of 40 minutes. The train weight involved was 240 tonnes, but as the brakes were partially applied this was the equivalent of operating at an all-up weight of 1,200 tonnes.

The first two prototypes appeared in 1978, and like many new Scammells before it and since, the Commander was to be the star commercial exhibit at the Birmingham NEC Motor Show. Understandably, the public likened it to the then current Foden Haulmaster range, for the basic cab unit was in fact a standard Motor Panels product. Cabs may never have been a stong Scammell concern, but this double-sleeper version did them proud and offered both a high degree of serviceability and a level of comfort which previously had not been considered as part of the Watford trademark.

Inside the cab there was no sign of a massive Scammell gearbox gate, for although the gear-shift may have had a lever, it was small and close to being insignificant, as was the parking brake control. Small it may have been, but that little gear-lever was the visual end of an entirely new concept of transmissions for Scammell, one which, like many of their previous ideas, was set to alter the whole thinking of the entire heavy-haulage industry.

The gearbox was a six-speed Allison CLBT 6061, imported from the USA, and the incorporation of a torque converter linked to an all-electric powershift meant that driving the new Scammell was a new experience.

The two 1978 prototypes differed in one main respect, namely their engines. Power outputs were similar, for the main parameter that the army had given Scammell was that the new transporter had to be capable of the basic performance demanded of any other commercial vehicle on the road. As the law at that time was imposing a minimum engine output of 6bhp per gross ton of the vehicle's weight when it was fully loaded, the engine output required for the Scammell was fairly easy to calculate. Battle tanks had come a long way since those first versions carried on the Pioneer, which weighed in at 15 to 20 tons, for the Chieftain and the new Challenger were to tip the scales between 55 and 65 tons. To this had to be added the unladen weight of the Commander roadtrain, which was 37.2 tons, so in round figures the all-up weight was about 100 tons, which, at 6bhp per ton, meant that an engine output of 600bhp was required.

The two types of engine used in the trials were the 26.1-litre Rolls-Royce V12, offering 625bhp plus 1,680lb ft of torque, and the Cummins KTA 600, which produced 600bhp. Both were to perform in a highly admirable manner, but the final choice in favour of the Rolls-Royce power pack was made mainly on the grounds of standardization, because this make of engine was also used in the battle tanks that the Commander was built to carry.

Sat behind the left-hand-drive steering wheel, the driver's eyes are 10 feet from the ground and are offered a commanding view of the road beyond the tapered glassfibre bonnet. With the Rolls-Royce engine burbling into life, getting the Commander into motion is simply a matter of notching the lever into first gear, releasing the park brake lever round its L-shaped gate and applying pressure to the throttle pedal, which is the one furthest to the right of the three pedals on the floor. Up-changes come in a fairly quick manner, with a green light glowing on the facia to indicate when it is possible. There is no clutch pedal to worry about, and the system also protects itself by refusing to change down if road/engine speed is too high. The pedal on the left is a gearbox retarder, an in-built transmission braking device to assist the main two-line air braking system.

The first eight of the Commanders, coupled to specially developed Crane Fruehauf Class 90 semi-trailers, were delivered to 414 Tank Transporter Unit, based at Bulford Camp in Wiltshire, during March and April 1984, while a similar batch went to 16 Tank Transporter Squadron in West Germany. To say the army was impressed is a bit of an understatement, for although the Commander was slightly longer, wider and heavier than the Antar it was phasing out, its performance was such that a whole day could be cut from a typical journey to South Wales that used to take the old Thornycroft three days to complete. With the problems of attaining maximum efficiency in tank movement, having a transporter that can go as quickly as this is a particular asset to any logistics department, even though it means using a vehicle 64 feet 3 inches long, 12 feet 2 inches wide and 12 feet 5 inches high.

The Commander was to perform well, perhaps too well, in fact, as the army found the new Scammell's appetite for work was insatiable. High speed with heavy weights prompted a rise in the temperature of the differential oil, so Watford had to make slight modifications in the back bogie to allow for cooler running.

For those who wanted to compare the new Scammell with other types of tank transporter, the opportunity was afforded when the Commander went to Tehran as a support vehicle for a British battle tank being tried out alongside other countries' military hardware. The trials for the tanks and their accompanying transporters were hard, but the Scammell was seen to perform exceptionally well. Its counterpart from behind the Iron Curtain, based on a vehicle of MAZ manufacture, did not do as well. It was running three to four hours behind the Commander and had to be accompanied by a group of foot soldiers, who were continually throwing water onto the vehicle to cool it down, so testing was the ground it had to cover.

Selling military vehicles is fairly straightforward in times of peace, but when Iran and Iraq went to war with each other, Scammell were effectively banned from trading with these countries for sales of the new Commander. Back on the domestic front, meanwhile, the problems of Scammell were linked to those caused by the recession in both haulage and heavy-haulage circles. But time moves on, and changes were once more to come Scammell's way as the booming 1970s led into the fighting 1980s.

At the lighter end of the range, Scammells changed very little from the time when the first production vehicles appeared in the 1920s until well into the post-war years. The tractive units had become a little broader in the beam, and pneumatic tyres had replaced the early solids, but the unmistakable, stark lines remained. The no-frills approach was disliked by many drivers, but the ability to withstand all sorts of abuse endeared these wagons to their operators. This example, DDW 161, was new to Wynns in 1941.

GPT 194 is seen on March 19, 1952 in this British Steel photograph, having only recently been compulsorily acquired from Fred Robinson of Stockton. Measuring 18ft in the well, the Gardner-powered Scammell was rated by Pickfords as a 20-tonner, but was soon to be replaced by a new Scammell of similar capacity, number 8086 (then M915), registered NYN 963. At this time, the vehicle was the second strongest machine based at the North Shore Goods Station depot on Norton Road, Stockton. Other vehicles based there were a 45-ton chain-drive Scammell, a 15-ton Maudslay low-loader, an AEC 4x4 Matador and two small artic Bedfords. The depot was transferred to Church Road in 1962, then finally closed in 1975, after operating road tankers only for its last three years.

Tom Hallett was a World War 1 soldier who, after demob, bought an ex-Army lorry for haulage work in and around London, obtaining his first A licence on their introduction in 1933. Scammells featured strongly in his fleet. Driver Jack Parker is pictured at the Bell Bar Cafe, *en route* from County Durham with a 16ft diameter fuel tank destined for Aveley, Essex. People at the Ford Motor Company plant were to remember well the arrival of this load, for it became entangled in some overhead cables and plunged the place into darkness for a couple of hours. The writing on the side of the load relates to a country and western song made famous by Lonnie Donnegan when he sang about the Rock Island Line.

John Silberman started business in 1946 and began to work very closely with Tom Hallett. On his retirement in the early 1950s, Tom sold his business, vehicles and licences to John, and eventually both the Hallett and the Silberman vehicles were to share the name Hallett Silberman, a trading title the Brent company still uses today. Working in concert, the small 25-ton Scammells were not afraid to have a go at anything, and there was about 80 tons all-up weight in this pull-push outfit. The 30-ton submarine engine being moved on this occasion was quite long and needed the use of the Crane 60-ton float for the haul from Chatham to Scotland. *Red Dragon* is the name on FYK 349, the leading tractor.

By 1955, the double split windscreen of the cab had been dropped for a single split, and the general line was starting to smooth out. Bent-Marshall bought the Meadows-engined NGF 120 from Pickfords around 1963, and two years later the Scammell was to be coupled to the 30-ton capacity King tandem-axle low-loader. Seen approaching the A12 near Chelmsford in a photograph taken by Michelin to illustrate the use of their metallic tyres, the Scammell, which was operated on a B licence, is carrying a 15-ton bulldozer. When sold by the operator, it was to be saved for preservation by a man from North London, who painted it in its original Pickfords colours and converted it to a ballast box tractor, a conversion carried out by many people. The trailer was refurbished and strengthened by the Essex operator, who still finds it fit for 40 to 45-ton loads.

Wrekin Roadways, too, favoured the ballast box tractor configuration. LRE 97 was an early requisition by David James on starting up operations after denationalization; the Scammell, hauling an ex-tank transporter, is carrying a crane trolley frame from the Horsehay Co Ltd. The coachlining carefully applied to the flat cab panels is a tradition carried on from an earlier era, and adds a touch of finesse to this strictly utilitarian old workhorse.

By the late 1950s, the 25-tonner had been given another facelift and a far more pleasing line to the cab. Hallett Silberman were to name the Gardner-powered 977 RMD *Red Robin II*, the triangular sign on the top of the cab being a company logo designed by their first foreman, a crusty old character called Bill Ward. As any engineer will tell you, one triangular steel section inserted upside-down within a similar section is particularly strong, and thus the symbol represented the company's ability to take extremely heavy loads. These Metal Propellers cracker columns that inched out of the works in Purley Way, Croydon, were an impressive sight, and a cause of some concern to the rose-growing neighbours who lived opposite the entrance.

In the early 1960s, the Highwayman cab reached the shape that was to see it into retirement. The radiator grille had not changed a great deal, and the steering wheel was still very much in an upright plane. Although the Leyland 600 and 680 engines, offering 125 and 150bhp, were standard fitment, many operators such as Wrekin Roadways were to favour Gardner's finest at that time, the 6LX-150. WUJ 450 heads up the similarly laden and well-remembered Foden MPT 527 *en route* to Corby with these 25-ton crane girders supported on strong ex-tank transporters. The Highwayman was to be sold to Talbot Plant Hire, at Telford, and later Liz Mason, a VAT inspector, was to save it for preservation.

Above: the Scammell Highwayman was used in both ballast box and articulated form, although this Ulster Transport method of hauling a semi-trailer with a fore carriage was apparently just a posed situation. Pickfords' Preston depot dealt with all traffic to and from Northern Ireland via Larne, using the Ulster haulier, later to be called Northern Ireland Carriers, to move their unaccompanied traffic. *Empire Cymric* was one of the early ferry boats used on this crossing which, later, were to be replaced by the similar type of Doric boats.

Opposite: Wrekin Roadways was one of the many heavy haulage operators who, even as late as 1969-70, preferred to opt for the long-established Highwayman rather than the more modern Scammell offerings. The Tetley operator did a great deal of work for the nearby Adamson-Alliance crane manufacturers, who were also known as The Horsehay Co, Adamson-Butterley and AB Cranes before they were closed in 1985. Driver Terry Whittaker had to take this 25-ton, 17ft 11in high load to BSC Llanwern in about 1971. Wrekin hired the Crane semi-trailer from Foulkes, of Wednesfield, to do the job, for it was quite a rare low-loader with a carrying area 30ft long.

Robert Wynns were another company who kept faith with the Highwayman for their heavier work, VDW 324 being one of a pair, consecutive with VDW 325 (fleet number 181), bought new to the fleet in 1960. This Peter Lee photograph, taken in the mid-1970s, shows the Scammell attending a traction rally event at Bristol. Its cargo was the sole Fowler saved for preservation from the days when Wynns had a fleet of 20 steam traction engines operating throughout the country. It was also the pride and joy of Arthur Matthews, who kept it in immaculate running order, Arthur having joined Wynns in the late 1920s. Peter Lee recalled the Scammell making a stop at Clifton Gorge, on the journey from South Wales, so that the Fowler could be fired up to produce a full head of steam by the time it arrived at the rally. Wynns were to donate the Fowler to Newport Corporation when they closed down operations in South Wales. It is currently kept at Tredegar House, and a group of enthusiasts ensures it still attends events in the Cardiff area, literally under its own steam.

The Crusader was originally built by Scammell in collaboration with the National Freight Corporation as a high-speed trunking vehicle to run at 32 tons gross. However, the natural tendency of Scammell for in-built strength soon saw the model used on the lighter side of heavy haulage operations. Chris Bennett's Rolls-Royce-powered four-wheeler was running at 42 tons gross when seen on Teesside in 1979. With the addition of another drive axle, the 6x4 Crusader became popular with people like Hills of Blackwell, who were keen to secure vehicles that were originally intended for export. Although only rated at 65 tons train weight, the Detroit-powered Scammell was running at 95 tons all-up weight when seen at Hartlepool in 1980, close to the delivery point of this crawler machine brought up from Kent.

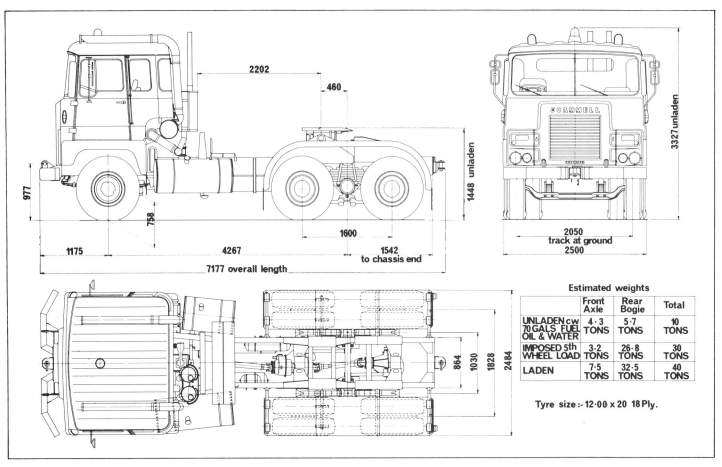

Estimated weights

	Front Axle	Rear Bogie	Total
UNLADEN cw 70 GALS FUEL OIL & WATER	4·3 TONS	5·7 TONS	10 TONS
IMPOSED 5th WHEEL LOAD	3·2 TONS	26·8 TONS	30 TONS
LADEN	7·5 TONS	32·5 TONS	40 TONS

Tyre size :- 12·00 x 20 18 Ply.

Wynns were one of the companies who advocated the official uprating of the Crusader. With their collaboration, Scammell were to strengthen the 6x4 chassis and slip in a lightweight Contractor rear bogie. The Wynns drawing above depicts a versatile vehicle capable of hauling 10 times its own weight. Dimensions are in millimetres. The vehicle was officially designated simply the 100-ton Crusader, although to many the machine was known as the Amazon, and Wynns were to replace some Crusader badging, even though Scammell did not wish them to do so. The *Commercial Motor* photograph opposite shows one of the first two 100-tonners to enter service with Wynns, at the 1977 Commercial Motor Show. Number 627 had the Rolls-Royce 290 engine and the 15-speed gearbox; it was registered YGS 384S and originally was based at the Manchester depot, while stablemate 626 was registered VUH 713S and went to Chasetown. Wynns were to run six of these 100-tonners in all, the original pair being renumbered 205 and 206 when the fleet was repainted under the name Wynns Heavy Haulage, which officially incorporated the vehicles of Wrekin Roadways.

Left: the Scammell factory photograph of the lone UK Samson depicts a fine looking machine. Pickfords fleet number M7052 was to be registered EYF 886J, being chassis number WHV 52007. The Samson was a standard 13ft-wheelbase 6x4 Crusader with an extra steering axle blended into the chassis. Its engine was the 9.25-litre Detroit 8V-71 two-stroke V8, which produced 290bhp at 2,100rpm and 805lb ft of torque. It went on the road in April 1971, and Pickfords were to work the vehicle long and hard, but it was not until 13 years and several owners later that the Samson was to show its true potential behind, rather than in front of, a massive load.

Right: it was in 1968 that the Army first mooted the replacement of the Thornycroft Antar tank transporter. Scammell's strategy adopted to meet the requirements was based on their own experience, which stretched back to 1932 and included the expertise brought with the Thornycroft staff amalgamation in 1970. In 1972-73 a dummy tractor unit, seen here and on the next two pages, was built as part of the concept study. A problem with the original design was revealed when engines of up to 800bhp were being considered, and it was necessary to remount the massive cooling group of radiators behind the cab rather than at the front of the bonnet. At this time, it was thought that the vehicle would be right-hand drive, and other interesting details include the novel spread-beam headlight arrangement.

As development of the tank transporter continued, two more mock-ups were built, illustrated here and on the following pages. Two variations of the front end and grille were tried, one of them close to what was to be the production version. The Commander was to be fitted with two fuel tanks, giving a total capacity of 908 litres (200 gallons approximately), and each tank could be isolated to feed the engine independently. Wheels were standardized and fitted with 14.00-24 tyres, while the front suspension consisted of two semi-elliptic leaf springs with dampers. Static test-rig work was undertaken to prove the cab, its mounting and the bonnet on simulated rough road and suspension test tracks taken from recordings of the MVEE test facilities.

The interior of the Commander was revealed as quite a plush working environment when compared to some previous Scammell offerings. The factory photographs here and overleaf show a cab designed as a double-sleeper or able to take five people in reasonable comfort. The park/secondary brake lever is the one closest to the floor, whilst the notched arrangement of the powershift electronic gear-change is clearly visible. Although there is no clutch pedal, the footbrake is supplemented by a gearbox retarder, which would allow both feet to be used if an emergency situation arose. A Bostrom suspension seat is fitted for the driver, which places his eyes about 10ft off the ground. The vehicle seen through the passenger window is an Explorer which was one of a batch of prototypes built about 1950 and bought back by Scammell for sentimental reasons from a dealer in War Department surplus near Bedford.

The Commander was designed very much as a complete articulated tank-transporter, although the original procurement was for a total of 125 tractive units and 117 semi-trailers; of these it was planned that 91 tractors and 83 semi-trailers would go to BAOR (British Army of the Rhine). The army still considers them as separate units and numbers them accordingly, but finding a Commander without its semi-trailer is rare. In this form, the Scammell weighs 21 tons 7 cwt, is 29ft 6in long, 10ft 4in wide, and the top of the flashing beacon is 11ft 9in from the ground. The horizontal drum hydraulic winch has a maximum single pull capacity of 20 tonnes, whilst the fitment of fairleads and rollers allows for rearward winching, thus permitting the Commander to self-unload.

121

The production version of the Commander, seen here undergoing proving trials, was a credit to all who had a say in its design or construction. With startling performance up to its top speed of about 40mph, the Commander was also intended to have all-terrain capability, which meant it was able to use gravel tracks — preferably graded and compacted to withstand the 100 tons of all-up weight. It was designed to withstand temperatures between minus 24 degrees and 43 degrees C, and be capable of operating at maximum efficiency anywhere up to 500 metres above sea-level with stop/start ability on gradients as steep as 1 in 5. The engine sump is fitted with a guard for protection, the ground clearance being measured as 13in. Scammell rate the maximum fording depth of rivers as 2ft 6in. All the Commanders based in the UK were to go to 414 Royal Corps of Transport, at Bulford, which in its distant past was known as the Hong Kong Mule Transport Troop.

52 KB 45

A173 BDP

With the arrival of the Commander, the long-serving Antars were soon disposed of. Staff Sergeant Greer, of the RCT, was on hand to record the last Antar leaving Ward Barracks, at Bulford, on January 30, 1985. The Antar, naturally being carried by a Commander, was *en route* to the British Car Auctions depot at Farnborough for disposal to the public. Just over 1,000 Antars were built at Thornycroft's works in Basingstoke, the British Army taking about 400 of them. The final Mk 3 version was fitted with the Rolls-Royce 16-litre C8 diesel, producing 333bhp, although the first army Antars were specified with the Rover V8 petrol engine. The canvas extension at the rear of the cab doubled both as protection for the recovery winch and as makeshift emergency sleeping quarters for the crew. The eventual destiny for the retired Antars seems very unsure, their being no big queue of potential buyers, although Millers of Preston have proved the potential of the 6x4 in civilian heavy haulage use, and the construction company DMD were to buy two for viaduct building work at Cardiff.

Although it may look aesthetically pleasing, the Scammell Commander is a vehicle built primarily for use in hostilities and rushing battle tanks to and from the combat zone is its main job. This photograph by Staff Sergeant Greer shows the Challenger, the latest battle tank of the British Army, in typical loading guise. The new Crane Fruehauf semi-trailer has replaced an old mixture of Dyson, Crane and Tasker units and offers a typical loading time of 10 minutes, half the time it used to take. The semi-trailer is 42ft 7in long, 12ft 2in wide and weighs 15 tons 17 cwt unladen, whilst the loading ramp angle is 27 degrees.

In peacetime, the Commander is a natural exhibit at army public relations events and can be asked to carry a variety of loads. This Tank Museum photograph, taken at Bovington in June 1985, shows the museum's Mark 5 tank of 1918 vintage — a veteran of the Battle of Amiens and still in running order — being loaded onto a Commander *en route* to Germany, where it took part in the Royal Tank Regiment standards parade before Her Majesty the Queen. Of note on the semi-trailer is how the loading ramps can be slid inboard to accept varying widths of vehicle.

5: STRENGTH IN NUMBERS

For hauling superweights, the big Contractors had certainly been impressive, although with a yearning for greater efficiency there would always be men like Sam Anderson who would try to improve a vehicle, even one which to many, including its manufacturer, was considered to be close to perfect.

Sam was an engineer who went from Pickfords to Wynns around 1959. He joined the Welsh operator as they were close to the end of the rejuvenating programme which converted Hall-Scott petrol-engined American Pacific M26 tank transporters into Welsh powerhouse heavy-haulage tractors. It had been a drastic change for these ex-army vehicles, but Sam Anderson was allowed to go even further in the re-engineering of *Challenger* by inserting a torque converter into the modified transmission. Rex Evans was this Pacific's regular driver, and even though it needed a second radiator to keep the oil cool, plus modifications to the speedometer, Rex was to like the vehicle, which was to prove good on fuel consumption.

The Contractor was eventually to supersede the Pacifics, although Sam was not entirely happy with the fluid flywheel in the semi-automatic transmission. A couple of them were blown up in Wynns vehicles, and starting this type of Scammell with a heavy load was invariably difficult. The Wynns board were to give Sam a free hand once they had seen his modifications to the 1969 version of *Dreadnought*, and he was keen to get to grips with one of Watford's best. It took the factory a little time to realize this man was serious. In fact they only believed him when he told the sales department that the next Contractor he was buying need not have an engine or a gearbox installed because these would be the first two items he was going to take out. But when Scammell put their minds to it the joint result was what many engineers believe to be the finest vehicle ever to squeeze out of the factory gates.

The Mark 2 Contractor was built purely for the home market as a heavy-haulage tractor, and only six were to be built. Appropriately, Wynns named their first one *Superior* when it was registered RWO 73R after making its first appearance on September 24, 1976 at the Commercial Show. On the road it made its first impression during one of the Wynns' 'bread runs' from GEC Stafford to the Pomona Dock at Manchester. The calculated all-up weight of the roadtrain was 540 tons, but the Mark 2 was allowed to work it on its own and it handled the weight with ease, which is not bad at all for a tractor which Scammell were still to plate at 240 tons train weight.

Outwardly, the Mark 2 does not look much different from the Mark 1, although the tape measure will confirm the visual hint that the cab and bonnet have been raised 7 inches to allow the massive Cummins 450 engine room to slip into the chassis. Using experience gleaned on Commander development, Scammell fitted the Allison gearbox and torque converter transmission, but this was of the fully automatic type rather than the electronic powershift of the military vehicle. A four-speed auxiliary box supplemented the main gearing, although Scammell were to warn Wynns only to use the lowest range for site work, never on the road, for the torque created from the incredibly low gearing coupled to the 450 Cummins would try to tear the vehicle in half.

On the road, the 450 Mark 2 gives itself away with a more throaty bark from the exhaust when compared to the smoother sound of the smaller 380 or 335 Cummins-powered Mark 1. In typical automatic fashion, once the short lever is pulled back into the 2-5 notch, progress is smooth and close to barnstorming, even with hundreds of tons on the back, instead of the characteristic jerky jolt predominant from the superseded semi-automatic gearbox.

There is very little in the way of improvement for the driver in the crew cab, however, and some drivers have been known to place a baulk of timber on the cab floor so that their feet can reach the awkwardly placed pedals. Scammell never courted good driver response from the Contractor's working environment, although few could deny its stength.

George Dowse recalled one heavy load under escort getting stuck on the the infamous Cut Bank, in Newcastle, with not enough power being available from the European-made tractor unit. The enterprising police escort spotted a Contractor running back solo and asked the driver if he would help out with a double head. Eager to assist, the Scammell driver hooked himself to the front and soon got into forward motion up the daunting incline, although all the Contractor succeeded in doing was to completely tear the entire front end out of the import and leave the rest of the outfit behind.

The six Mark 2s apart, the days of the big Scammell were numbered as hauliers started to look elsewhere for something more practical to tackle a bigger variety of work and perhaps to be more driver-acceptable. Scammell had suffered in consequence of their parent Leyland being robbed of development time and money to search for replacements for the dated Ergomatic concept, but in the early 1980s the long-awaited first examples of the T43 and T45 ranges appeared. Leyland were to name their first models the Landtrain and Roadtrain, although strangely Scammell went against tradition

by simply marketing their stronger derivatives under the bland descriptive numbering of S24 and S26, rather than conjuring up new names for them.

Those following the fortunes of Scammell would also have noticed a slight change in their name from the 1922 version of Scammell Lorries to the current Scammell Motors. Enquiring into this revealed it was not a high-ranking decision of the full board, but simply down to an administrative error. It is reported that one of the secretaries was preparing some new letterheads for the Leyland Group which listed all the relevant companies that had been absorbed. The list read Leyland Motors, Albion Motors, Guy Motors . . . so when it was Scammell's turn it seemed sensible to add the word 'Motors' to it, and at the slip of a typewriter key, Scammell Lorries moved into history.

The men on the shop floor had little time to concern themselves about minor administrative errors like this; they were more worried about their future working prospects as the Leyland conglomerate shrank into line with the recession of international truck markets. Watford had always championed themselves on flexibility, and as the 1980s stretched out this approach meant that production of the Leyland Group's premier vehicles was entrusted to Scammell. The three eight-wheeler chassis of the 1970s — Mammoth Major, Octopus and Routeman — were to evolve into a Watford-built Leyland Constructor, whilst the top-rated 38-tonner 6x2 general haulage tractor unit was also a Scammell product. These were to come off the production line intermingled with bonneted vehicles which may have looked outwardly identical, but would be badged either Leyland Landtrain or Scammell S24.

Finding out what goes into the finished product can sometimes be difficult, but George Dowse set about such research when he bought through the trade a machine that Watford had difficulty in accepting existed. George runs a specialist recovery business from the north side of the Tyne Tunnel, at North Shields, and looking for something with a bit of strength he bought what was to become SCN 779Y. The vehicle, which had only 11,000 kilometres on the clock, had stood for 18 months, so even the door and bonnet hinges were seized solid. There was no badging or chassis plate on the machine, which had been used on experimental braking development work, but George's practised eye picked out a Contractor chassis and 40-ton bogie, Himalayan hubs, Marathon-Crusader-type Alford-Alder front axle and Contractor exhaust system. The Cummins and nine-speed Fuller transmission was adorned with a Leyland/Albion Clydesdale-type cab, chopped and modified to accept a long glassfibre bonnet and metal mudguards.

It took 11 months of painstaking labour to ready the machine for the road, which included putting an extra 4 feet into the original wheelbase, but once at work the Scammell-badged vehicle was to show its true potential in a strange offshoot to recovery work, that of assisting stricken mobile cranes. The weight of these engineering masterpieces can exceed 100 tons in standard running form, but George and his *Iron Horse* have built up a national reputation of good service in being able to drag these masses back for repair. The Geordie thinks highly of his hybrid, even though he admits having regular conversations with the Cummins-powered machine to coax her through some testing situations.

This prototype and others like it have shown that even though Scammell have moved on into the 1980s, their new range is a simple development based round proven pieces. No harder test, which was passed with flying colours, could have been provided for the bonneted model than the rebuilding programme undertaken in the Falklands, which saw 79 of these tippers operated by Laing-Mowlem-ARC, working 23 hours a day for 2½ years and normally running 50% overloaded when hauling crushed rock products all over the island.

Across the Atlantic, in Africa, the S24/Landtrain range was fighting hard to keep the long-established markets built up on Super Beavers and Hippos, although it was to be the forward-control, flat-fronted S26 that was to prove more acceptable in the ever-changing fickleness of truck sales. Even stranger was the fact that in South Africa, due to import regulations, some Scammells were fitted with the V8 turbo twin Mercedes-Benz engine, but gave better fuel consumption than the identically powered comparable German-built truck that cost 15% more

to buy than the English machine.

When the law allowed, Scammell were to recommend fitment of the internationally accepted Cummins engines for these export models, and fitment of the Jake Brake was always advocated. Although many trucks were fitted with a floor-mounted exhaust brake switch as standard, which created back pressure and slowed the vehicle down by means of a butterfly-type flap in the exhaust system, the Jacobs engine brake took things a great deal further. Once the system was switched into one of the three different braking modes, lifting the foot from the accelerator pedal brought the Jake Brake into immediate operation. The system worked by upsetting the traditional engine cycle in that as the fuel intake was cut off, the exhaust valves were lifted so that no form of power stroke could be made. With the engine virtually stalling itself, it was the momentum of the vehicle that was needed to keep the crankshaft rotating. The effect of all this was that the loss of energy used to turn over the engine slowed the vehicle down without recourse to the foundation air brakes. The engine brake may have added a loud distinctive bark to the exhaust noise, but its performance was phenomenal, although drivers had to be on their toes to switch it off prior to coming to a halt to save the engine cutting out completely.

Back in the UK, the Cummins was regularly specified, although again it was the Rolls-Royce engine that was favoured in yet another military contract, which was only finalized in December 1986. For three years prior to that, Scammell had been in a head-to-head confrontation with the Paccar-owned Foden company as both firms' vehicles were put on trial by the army following the acceptance of a concept known as DROPS.

Demountable Rack Offloading and Pick-Up System was the full title of what was to totally revolutionize the army's movement of ammunition and other packaged equipment over long distances. Once loaded onto flat racks, the cargo need never be manhandled again as the self-contained DROPS vehicles were so equipped to pick up or unload without recourse to any other means. The flat racks were based on the dimensions of a standard 20-foot ISO container and could be carried either by rail or by truck. The physical transfer, however, of the flat rack from rail truck to Scammell did require the DROPS vehicle to pick up some separate container handling gear, although in all other respects, deposit or retrieval of their charge was to be exceptionally quick.

The army decided they would require two distinct types of vehicle, the first described as Medium Mobility, to be used mainly on built-up roads, but also able to cope with some cross-country work. The Improved Medium Mobility vehicles were expected to tackle more difficult terrain, and for this work Scammell initially offered the 6x6 S26 chassis, an 8x6 being the Scammell vehicle on trial for MM work.

Foden, however, put up the 8x6 as an IMM, and although Scammell were later to offer an eight-wheeler for this work, the eventual order for the 400 IMM vehicles went to Sandbach Engineering. Scammell, however, came out with the lion's share of the vehicle contract, for they won the order to supply 1,500 MM vehicles, the first of which was due to enter service in 1989.

The S26 has kept Scammell in the forefront of public attention, and in the late 1980s it even seems to have ousted the S24 as the leading Watford machine. Many may shake their heads in disbelief at this observation, because died-in-the-wool enthusiasts feel that the S26 is not really a true Scammell for it does not have a bonnet. But the star exhibit from Watford at the 1986 Motor Show, described as their International Heavy Hauler, was a rather special S26. Its 50.40 designation meant that the 6x4 unit could gross close to 50 tonnes weight, having 400bhp and being capable of 300 tonnes train weight operation. Its C51 full-width sleeper cab, which was raised and extended to include a fridge, cooker and sink, ranks with the best of the opposition and perhaps the only thing stopping the new S26 heavy-hauler taking the industry by storm is the numerous older Scammells still working hard for their living.

The latest acquisition of Dow Mac Concrete, at Eaglescliffe, in 1986 was a 35-years-old 6x6 Explorer. This tractor may have been used for internal work only, but shunting around anything up to 20 railway trucks at a time was not leisurely work, even though its original petrol engine had been replaced with a Leyland 680 diesel.

At the same time, hauling even heavier weights on the road in the Southampton area were two old Scammells owned by Tony Kimber, but on sub-contract work to Shamara Heavy Haulage. In 1983, Tony had rescued the lone 1970 Scammell Samson from the prospect of being cut up, and after a year's restoration, the eight-wheeler, reregistered Q362 NTR, was put to work pushing one of the strangest frame trailers ever seen. Built by the Warrington Wheel Company specifically for Pirelli, the trailer carries up to 120 tons of cable between Eastleigh and Southampton Docks. No modern aids are provided on this load carrier as it was built to be push-steered from the rear as well as being pull-steered from the front on the haul along the South Coast. The Kimber Samson has proven itself as the only vehicle fit for this strange task, its twin-steering front axles retaining more grip on the road than the 6x4 Contractor, which can be dragged sideways by the momentum of the strange yellow load carrier.

In early 1986, Tony was to buy BCN 318V, a 6x4 Contractor, to head up this roadtrain, although that registration number, like the Q-plate on the Samson, concealed the true age of the Scammell. In fact, it started work for Pickfords in November 1967, when it was registered SYO 386F, and the combined performance of these two old girls in moving over 250 tons all-up weight at their age is a proud reflection of the workmanship of Scammell.

Rarely is anything taken for granted in the truck-building industry. The destiny of the Leyland truck empire seemed in doubt as 1986 gave way to 1987, following talks with General Motors, then rumours about an involvement with Paccar of America (already controllers of Foden), followed by questions in the House about a proposed takeover by the Dutch DAF concern. Then came confirmation that the DAF solution was the one chosen, with Scammell's future not entirely clear, but however that fate unfolds, Watford's pedigree is long-established and unquestionable, and many justifiably believe that construction of supertrucks at that Tolpits Lane factory should never be allowed to cease.

RWO 73R was the first Mark 2 Scammell Contractor to be built and Wynns named the machine *Superior*. It was given the original fleet number of 602 and then renumbered 126 in the Wynns Heavy Haulage listings. It made its first appearance on September 24, 1976, although this David Jacobs photograph was taken about two years later. Driver Roger Banfield is on his way from Edmonton to Tilbury with a Cryoplants cold box destined for eventual delivery to the British Steel plant at Redcar, on Teesside. Not a great deal of weight, but about 20ft wide and 20ft high, and Wynns engineers have applied strengtheners to the load so that both it and its passenger, Tony Williams, can be carried in end suspension manner on a pair of Nicolas four-row bogies.

Pickfords were to take delivery of Mark 2 Contractors numbers 2 and 3 in the guise of XUU 919T and XUU 925T. This Norman Burniston photograph, taken on Cardwell Road, Gourock, shows the technique that the haulier had to use to cross a rather weak railway bridge. The inner stator core was being moved from Inverkip Power Station, near Glasgow, to NEI Parsons, on Tyneside, for repair. The all-up weight of the complete roadtrain is close to 500 tons, and the Mark 2 has a 150-ton MAN on the front for assistance. In January 1983, regular driver David Ginn was to demonstrate what 919T could really handle when he surmounted single-handed the testing Sheffield inclines to complete a haul into Davey McKee when the scales would have shown 450 tons being moved by that single 450 Cummins. Pickfords' general heavy haulage manager, John Banks, has seen many feats in his time, but that show of consummate power and strength was to fill him with awe.

Wynns' *Revenge*, registered DBF 134Y, was the last Mark 2 to be built, being bought by the haulier as one of a pair, the other one being registered DBF 133Y; at the time, their individual price tag was £120,000. Driver Roger Colcombe is seen just outside Guildford in this Surrey Police photograph taken in April 1983. Trailer number W1001 is carrying a 155-ton GEC transformer collected from Chessington, on the outskirts of London, and destined for Mannington sub-station, near Ringwood, on the Hampshire/Dorset border. Due to a weak bridge at Guildford, the Wynns outfit was forced off the main A3 road and obliged to take a major diversion; quite a headache for Surrey Police abnormal loads officer Jenny Tuffs, although such strange routing would become a thing of the past after April 1987, when that particular bridge was scheduled to be strengthened.

Into the 1980s, the six Mark 2s apart, the sun was setting on the general use of the Scammell Contractor. Many hauliers began looking elsewhere for a vehicle which could be more practicable for a wider variety of large and small loads, with the possible bonus that it could be more driver-acceptable. This Robert Price photograph, taken on March 9, 1976, shows Roger Binfield on the way to Croydon, following a circuitous journey to cross London which included a ride on the ro-ro ship from Tilbury to Kingsnorth. *Resolute*, hauling Crane 12-axle trailer number 999, was eventually disposed of by the newly formed consortium of Econofreight United, and went to a dealer in Ripley, Derbyshire. It was soon to be put back to work by Roger Harris, running Abnormal Load Engineering out of Stafford.

The factory presented the S24 range in prototype form during 1980, effectively a Scammell-strengthened derivative of the T43 Leyland Landtrain. Offered in either load-carrying or load-hauling form, the six-wheelers were built to work up to a possible 300 tonnes train weight operation. The key factor of the S24s was the standardization of components across the range. The premier offering, shown in the centre of this picture, is fitted with a separate sleeper pod, although access can be gained from the back of the three-seater cab, which also sports an air conditioning unit on top. The low-profile 24-20.5 Pilote sand tyres are more at home on unmade ground, quite a lot of noise being generated when they run on conventional road surfaces. First versions of the super heavyweights were fitted with a Spicer gearbox coupled to a Brockhouse torque converter.

Stewart and Maxwell Ward were early purchasers of the S24, their KCU 520X being a fine example of the range, still smart after five years of hard service with the County Durham plant operator. The resplendent condition of the vehicle, maintained by regular driver Tony Ayre, caught the eye of the pop group *Saxon*, who were to hire the S24 to go to Spain and use it there in a video promoting their latest record. The NTE 350 turbocharged Cummins-powered Scammell has a 15-speed Fuller gearbox, with 10 main and five super-low speeds, being rated for 120 tons operation. The rear axles are rated at 18 tonnes each, while the front axle is a 9-tonne heavy-duty Kirkstall. The sleeper box was made by Able-Body, of Joplin, Missouri.

Econofreight were to run two ballasted S24s for a variety of road and construction site work. A516 HVN, dwarfed by an Amoco platform, opposite, had a conventional engine-gearbox and normal clutch type of transmission, and was rated for 150 tons train weight. XTM 546X, above, was a version fit for 300 tonnes operation. It was run for quite a long period without any form of permanent box to carry its ballast weights, but once there was time to spare the vehicle from operational work, the Scammell was fitted with sleeping accommodation the like of which had never before been seen on the UK heavy haulage stage. The S24 staked its claim as fleet flagship when working up at Mossmorran, but is seen in this Tom Llewellyn photograph a lot closer to home, reversing up the testing Billingham Bank on February 24, 1985. Volvo RDC 955X is at the other end of this Air Products box, going in the right direction, this strange manoeuvre being adopted rather than trying the acute left turn at the bottom of the bank. This stretch of road is known by some heavy haulage followers as Jemison's Folly, following the incident where Bill's big Contractor had to be double-headed by an ICI Land-Rover.

As an articulated prime mover, the S24 was to be coupled to a large variety of semi-trailers, none more stange than the wide-spread eight-row Cometto that KZ 6882 is hauling, left. Dales Freightways, of Auckland, New Zealand, were also to run KZ 6881, the torque converter-equipped Scammells operating either in articulated or ballasted form. The Crane Fruehauf semi-trailer below is of more conventional size, being coupled to one of the two S24s operated out of Hinckley Point Power Station, on the Somerset coastline. This CEGB outfit carries about 5 tons of spent nuclear fuel elements in specially designed flasks, which have 14½in thick steel walls, on the short road haul to the Bridgwater railhead. The laden weight of each flask is 55 tons. Plated for 100 tons train weight and powered by the Cummins NTE 350 engine, both Scammells are fitted with the HT750 DRD Allison fully automatic gearbox.

By the time the Super Constructor came up for retirement in 1981, it had developed into one of the most versatile all-terrain, high-mobility vehicles, and could be produced as a flatbed oilfield truck, an off-road tractor or a military recovery vehicle. The high-floatation tyres helped to make it look distinctly mean at the same time. The recovery version combined a 25-ton winch — which could pull a heavy tank up a 30-degree slope with ease — and a 10-ton crane; a massive pivoted spade could hold the vehicle when winching, and retracting jacks were fitted to stabilize the Scammell during cranage operations. The Super Constructor's transmission had not changed since the early 1960s, still being the Self-Changing Gears semi-automatic gearbox, although the Rolls-Royce engine had been developed to produce 275bhp (gross).

The place in the Scammell catalogue formerly occupied by the Super Constructor was to be taken over by the 6x6 version of the S24, adaptable, like its predecessor, to a variety of roles from flatbed truck (above left) to recovery tractor (left). Perhaps the new vehicle was blander in appearance, but there had been an improvement in efficiency. The 6x6 S24 was also offered in the role of articulated tank transporter prime-mover, right. It may not have had the startling on-road performance of the Commander, but at half the price it was at home in terrain not really suited for its more powerful stablemate. The machine was a direct derivative of the civilian range, with the standard NTE 350 engine. Transmission went through a 15-speed Fuller RTX 14615 gearbox, and a hydraulic twin 20-tonne line pull winch was fitted as standard to retrieve inoperative equipment. The driving compartment was normally the standard three-man day cab, air-conditioned if required, although Scammell offered optional crew or sleeper versions and a choice between left or right-hand drive.

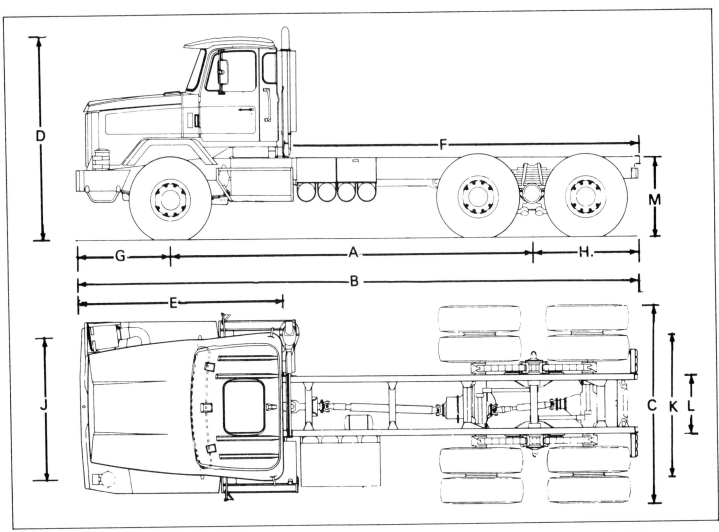

Scammell S24 6x4 heavy duty on/off road truck/tractor chassis. Dimensions in millimetres. **A**: wheelbase 4,734 or 5,410. **B**: overall length 7,659 or 8,335. **C**: overall width 2,856. **D**: overall height (unladen) 3,078. **E**: bumper to cab back 3,034. **F**: cab to end of frame 4,625 or 5,301. **G**: front overhang 1,385. **H**: rear overhang 1,540. **J**: front track 2,046. **K**: rear track 2,044. **L**: frame width 864. **M**: frame height (at centre line of bogie) unladen 1,184, laden 1,138. **N**: bogie spread 1,600. **Tyres** G.20 or 14.00-20.

These early publication drawings illustrating the top-of-the range Scammell models pinpoint immediately one critical difference in dimensions between them. With a width of 2.856 metres, the bonneted S24, left, does not comply with the basic UK Construction and Use regulations; this does not debar it, however, from 'Special Types' work. In contrast, the slimmer 2.491 metres width of the smoother-fronted Roadtrain look-alike S26, right, means that, being under 2.5 metres, it is theoretically available for both Special Types and Construction and Use regulated traffic. The unladen weights of both basic chassis are very close to the 12 tonnes mark. The engine in both cases is the 14-litre six-cylinder Cummins NTE 350 diesel, turbocharged and aftercooled to produce 350bhp gross, 326bhp net, at 2,100rpm. A variety of transmission options is available to suit different operating requirements, and the available performance in terms of speed, load hauling capacity and gradient climbing ability varies according to which is fitted, but with the standard back axle ratios of 7.74:1 for the S26 and 8.77:1 for the S24, maximum geared speeds are 72kph (45mph) and 66kph (41mph) respectively.

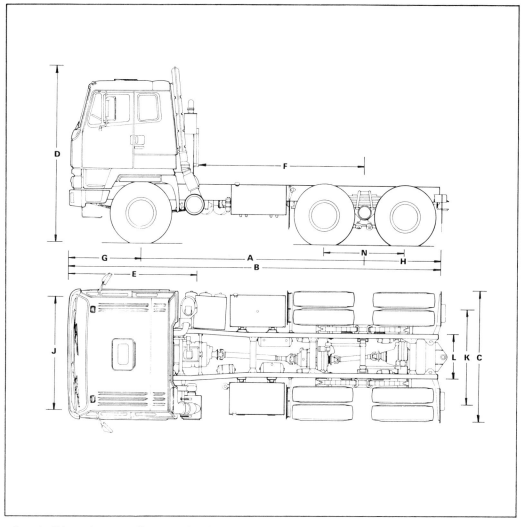

Scammell S26 6x4 heavy duty tractor chassis. Dimensions in millimetres. A: wheelbase 4,500. B: overall length 7,440. C: overall width 2,491. D: overall height (unladen) 3,491. E: bumper to maximum body buildline 2,585. F: maximum body buildline to centre line of bogie 3,325. G: front overhang 1,410. H: rear overhang 1,675. J: front track 2,073. K: rear track 1,854. L: frame width (at rear) 860. M: frame height (at centre line of bogie) unladen 1,185, laden 1,134. N: bogie spread 1,600. **Tyres** 12.00-20.

146

Although outwardly the S24 and S26 appear as two distinctively different units, under the skin they are in fact very similar. The micrometer would reveal that the S24 has a slightly heavier frame as well as its obviously longer wheelbase, but the Hill and Morgan vehicles seen above and opposite share the same engine specifications, transmission and 150-ton rating. Hill's driver, Nobby Brown, is seen in June 1985 about to deliver a 54-ton Centurion tank to the National Army War Museum in Chelsea. The semi-trailer being used on this journey from Ludgershall was a Walker three-axle. The Tony Morgan driver was Doug Randall, and he is seen with mate Ken Harry in the Abergavenny area on April 19, 1985. The Bristol Channel cutter *Olga* being carried on the 110-ton capacity Taskers semi-trailer was found in a dock at Maldon, Essex. Built in Cornwall, the vessel spent most of its working life sailing out of Barry and it was brought back to South Wales on behalf of the Swansea Maritime Museum. This S26's extended cab accommodation plan was to form the basis of the similar factory version offered in 1986. Morgans sold the outfit in 1986 because it was rather big for their normal traffic, and it joined the predominantly ERF fleet of Brian Rodwell's Leicester Heavy Haulage, at Loughborough.

Following the amalgamation of Econofreight, Wynns and Sunters in May 1986, the combined fleet was painted in the blue-and-white featured as standard on Econofreight's vehicles. During November and December 1986, the hauliers were particularly busy throughout the UK with one of their more prestigious jobs, the road-haul of five similar sections from ITM Thornaby to ITM Normanby, on Teesside, these being recorded in the sequence of pictures on these pages by the camera of Dennis Harris. The first two loads, moved in convoy on November 16, 1986, saw a variety of Scammells in use, all easily identifiable and some still in their previous paint scheme. With a train weight in excess of 400 tons, XTM 546X had NAJ 103P as constant pusher at the rear. For the 2-mile climb from Marton Cross Roads to the top of Dixons Bank, at Nunthorpe, Terry Thompson headed-up the duo in the ballasted S26, B327 KVN. Heading-up that combination to ease onto the soft construction site was Ken Bickerton in YAX 165T, the Contractor originally having been adorned with the nameplate *Buccaneer*, this being the second tractor driven by Ken on this particular day. A fortnight later, the Middlesborough-based vehicles were all being used at Stanlow, so Teesside was blessed with the barnstorming performance of the Stafford-based Mark 2 Contractor DBF 134Y, driven by Mick Nagginton. His pusher was XAX 512T, but with a journey time 2 hours shorter than the previous 8 hours of the first loads, it brought smiles to the escorting police motorcycle team of Tony Storry, Peter Ogden, Dereck Walton and Brian Laverick. The Mark 2 completed the run without any form of double-heading, although a total of three tractors were hung on the back by move supervisor Roy Brandley for the long harrowing descent down Ormesby Bank.

The DROPS contract — Demountable Rack Offloading and Pick-up System — was the revolutionary new way the Ministry of Defence envisaged the British Army moving packed cargo, like ammunition, in the 1990s. The concept of having self-contained vehicles able to load and unload either themselves or their respective drawbar trailers with standard NATO pallets or flat racks was based originally on a civilian system of hydraulic lifting gear for moving heavy skips of debris and rubbish. The flat racks are loaded or unloaded by a right-angled arm mounted behind the cab. Actuated by hydraulics driven from the power take-off, the arm hauls the load onto rails on the carrying vehicle chassis. The same hydraulics can also be used to push or pull the flat rack onto a drawbar trailer. Running with a trailer, the DROPS vehicle can carry a payload of 30 tonnes out of its all-up weight of 50 tonnes.

The Ministry of Defence identified two distinct types of vehicle to be used on the DROPS contract. The Medium Mobility vehicle would be used mainly on built-up roads, but would be expected to tackle some cross-country work, while the Improved Medium Mobility vehicle would be able to tackle the more difficult terrain. For the latter slice of the contract Scammell offered the Ministry their 6x6 S26, and the 8x6 S26 was put forward as the Medium Mobility vehicle. Foden, who were Scammell's main competitors, put forward an eight-wheeler for both types of work. Although Scammell were later to revise their IMM vehicle and resubmit an 8x6, they felt in hindsight that this was why they lost the eventual contract for the 400 IMM vehicles, which went to Foden.

In December 1986, after three years of trials, Scammell were awarded the contract to supply 1,500 Medium Mobility 8x6 S26 vehicles, which would be fitted with the Multilift Handling system, delivery to commence in 1989 and to be completed in 1993. The Scammell S26 was to be fitted with the Perkins Rolls-Royce Eagle engine developing 350bhp at 2,100rpm. The foremost steering axle and the rear two axles are driven through the HT750 DRD Allison five-speed fully automatic gearbox, coupled to a lockable torque converter, so driving these very impressive new monsters should not be particularly difficult.

Not built to carry a great deal of cargo, this S26 was not even badged as a Scammell for it was Leyland France's entry in the 1984 Paris-Dakar Rally; it was registered A352 MPP simply to get it across the Channel. The rally attracts up to 600 competitors, who drive trucks, cars and motorcycles away from the start at the Palace of Versailles. The 21-day event, which is arguably the world's toughest contest of its kind, covers 6,800 miles through France, Algeria, Niger, Mali, Mauritania and Senegal. DAF of Holland have been the most exciting commercial entrant to the event, their 1983 entry being a 4x4 machine which had both a cab and an engine at each end of the vehicle.

Scammell were very much aware that not every tank movement needed the power of the Commander, nor the all-terrain capability of the all-wheel-drive S24. The civilian-derived S26 was a far cheaper unit for the movement of battle tanks, armoured fighting vehicles or other military equipment on built-up highways. The standard cab came in either left or right-hand drive form, along with twin-sleeper facilities. The engine/transmission was identical to the cross-country S24, being the NTE 350 Cummins and 15-speed Fuller manual gearbox. A winch was also fitted, but this was of the single 20-tonne line pull horizontal-drum type. Fully loaded, the S26 transporter was capable of maintaining a continuous operational speed of 38mph, with a gradient capability of 19%.

Above right: Scammell were to revive the title Mountaineer as a tradename for some S26s that were built to be sold by one budding entrepreneur in the United States, although at the time of writing this contract had not been finalized. Another order, showing the flexibility of approach adopted by Watford, was for 50 S26 aircraft refuellers. The 6x4 vehicles were fitted with 22.5in wheels on low-profile tyres in order to drop their running height as they had to be capable of being squeezed onto a Hercules transport plane, right. Scammell's engineers were to conceive a method of clamping down the vehicle's cab and suspension so that crucial inches could be saved when loading.

Contrasts. This gleaming S26 was arguably the star exhibit of the 1986 Motor Show. The original artist's drawings of this vehicle saw it named Conveyor, but the title was not to be translated onto the final vehicle, which was simply designated the 50.40. The numbering meant 50 tonnes gross (49 tonnes was actually recommended) and 400bhp coming from the Cummins NTE 400 engine. The transmission was the ZF Transmatic, with 16 separate ratios available from the Ecosplit gearbox working through a torque converter. The extended C51 full-width sleeper cab incorporated a fridge, cooker and sink. Scammell rated their new heavy hauler as fit for 300 tonnes all-up operation, and it was set to take the world by storm . . .

. . . were it not for all the other, older Scammells still hard at work. The latest acquisition of Dow Mac Concrete at Eaglescliffe in 1986 was this 1951 6x6 Explorer. Fitted with non-standard bumpers, the Leyland 680-powered vehicle was used on internal work only; pulling and pushing up to 20 railway trucks at a time was how it earned its keep a mere 35 years after it first saw the light of day.

Still hard at work in North West Scotland in 1986 were PNT 901R and UDU 59W. Peter Sunter had sold these two 6x4 Mark 1 Contractors, when he was running Wynns Heavy Haulage at Stafford, to make room for the last two Mark 2 Contractors to be built. Both these Scammells had started life with Wrekin Roadways, PNT 901R having fleet number 31 and UDW 59W allocated the Wrekin number of 38. Highlands Fabricators are based at Nigg Bay, Ross-shire, being a consortium jointly owned by Brown Root (UK) Ltd and Wimpey International Ltd. Hi-Fab started production in 1972, their biggest construction being the 40,000-tonne British Petroleum Magnus jacket built in 1982. The fabricator uses the Scammells for site work only, and here, about 600 tonnes in this part of Conoco's revolutionary tension-leg platform hull are being supported on Nicolas axles. The Contractors may not get very far, but their current owners still expect them to move loads of 1,600 tonnes between them.

Trumpeting the longevity of the Scammell on the south coast of England is this regular sight witnessed by people in the Southampton area. The Pirelli-Shamara-Kimber-Scammell roadtrain has been working between the two Pirelli factories at Eastleigh and Southampton Docks since 1984. The double-cranked frame trailer was built by the Warrington Wheel Company specifically to the Pirelli design. The specially produced cable comes straight from the production area at Eastleigh and rotates itself onto the large bobbin mounted in the centre of the trailer. The trailer, weighing in at 67 tons unladen, was designed to carry up to 120 tons of payload, lacks any modern aids, and was built to be push/steered from the back as well as being pull/steered from the front. The only tractor that was able to control the fierce sideways momentum at the back of the trailer was the lone UK Samson that Tony Kimber rescued from Cranes & Commercials, a dealer in Southampton. It took close to a year to put the 8x4 Scammell back on the road; running in ballasted form, it rocks the scales to 40 tons. The first Shamara Contractor used to head-up this run was XUP 999F, but in January 1986, Tony Kimber's BCN 318V took over this testing haul, which involves a combined all-up weight to be moved of 260 tons.

On August 9, 1986, Tony Kimber's 240-ton Contractor took time out from hauling the distinctive Pirelli trailer to move *Endeavour*, one of the last J class yachts, built for racing in 1934. For about seven years, the partially refurbished vessel, which was valued in seven-figure numbers, had sat immobile on its cradle at Calshot Spit, and although many thought that the Kimbers could not move it in situ, as the original carriage wheels had fallen off, the slow control of Mike Hughes at the landlubbing wheel made them eat their words. With 70 tons of lead in the keel, the 130ft long steel-hulled yacht weighed approximately 150 tons, so to ensure traction on the move, the Scammell was ballasted up to 51½ tons, while a fire hose was utilized to water down the ground as the cradle slid over it.